*I pray you know & feel the love
of the Father & are encouraged —
by our story! Blessings,*

Hope in the Midst

*Kelly,
I pray these words will
encourage & our stories
will bring hope.
Psalm 102:1-2 'Hear my
prayer, O Lord...'*

Hope in the Midst

30 Devotions of Comfort and Inspiration

Marianne Takacs
&
Mary Rose Takacs

WestBow
PRESS
A DIVISION OF THOMAS NELSON

WestBow Press books may be ordered through booksellers or by contacting:

WestBow Press
A Division of Thomas Nelson
1663 Liberty Drive
Bloomington, IN 47403
www.westbowpress.com
1-(866) 928-1240

ISBN: 978-1-4497-2352-1 (sc)
ISBN: 978-1-4497-2351-4 (ebk)

Library of Congress Control Number: 2011914361

Printed in the United States of America

WestBow Press rev. date: 09/27/2011

Contents

Hope Can Be Found

To our guys,
Randy and Josh.
Your love and support carry us through.
Thank you for your constant prayers
and for believing in us.

I waited patiently for the Lord;
he turned to me and heard my cry.
He lifted me out of the slimy pit,
out of the mud and mire;
he set my feet on a rock
and gave me a firm place to stand.
He put a new song in my mouth,
a hymn of praise to our God.
Many will see and fear
and put their trust in the Lord.

—Psalm 40:1-3

Acknowledgments

First and foremost, thanks to our Savior, Jesus Christ, without whom this book would undoubtedly not have been written. Whether facing the battles of illness or during the retelling of our stories, You have been our shield of protection, our perseverance when the days were exhausting, our hope when we had none, and our joy that brought strength. You are all sufficient at all times. We love You above all else.

Mary Rose and I know beyond a shadow of a doubt the sharing of our stories would not have come together without the help of many people. Our thanks go out to friends and family members who encouraged us and prayed us through this project.

From Marianne: Randy, you are my biggest supporter, without whom I would not have considered this undertaking. You know me like no other, except my Lord. Thank you for your constant love and willingness to be there always for both Mary Rose and me. Your ever-present humor has brought a smile to my face more times than I can count! Thank you for encouraging me through the years when I wasn't sure how to continue on during the illness. Jeremiah, J, my "favorite son," your humor and gentle heart are the parts I love most about you. Our Barbie doll antics left me with laughter and joy so often! Thanks for being you and knowing how to bring laughter to the otherwise awkward situations of life!

Rosie, my princess, you are the daughter I always prayed for. Your warm heart, generous and adventurous spirit, constant love, and unending desire for coffee (only matched by mine!) are only a few of the things I love about you. Your love of and dedication to your Savior, your family, and your (soon-to-be) husband are unrivaled. I would not have even considered the writing of this book if you had not felt the same desire and passion for it.

Betsy, my sister and friend, your humor and views on life lift me beyond the here and now. Thank you for being one of my biggest supporters! Mom Takacs, your appreciation for family and dedication to its preservation have taught me many things. Thank you for your faithful service to and love of our family.

My thanks go out to those who have given of themselves to help our family during the worst years of Mary Rose's illness. Charlena, you have been an incredible friend! Whether in the duration of fighting the Lyme or in the process of writing a book, your friendship and constant support are always there for me. Leslie, my sweet sister in the Lord, you have my heart's appreciation and enduring thanks. The truths we've shared and the storms weathered together with God as our constant have helped me grow in ways I never thought possible. Carleen, my sounding board, your words of comfort and uplifting got me through many a sad moment. Keep your sense of humor—"It's critical!" Carol, without your faithfulness as my own personal laundress for an entire year, I surely would have lost my mind! Dale and JoAnne, all those yummy pies and dozens of meals were a frequent source of relief to our exhausting days; thank you. Joni, early on, when I desperately needed wisdom, God put you into my life for a time. Thank you for your kind words and the truths shared from God's Word. The many cards sent through Joni and Friends remain as treasures tucked away in the attic now.

From Mary Rose (Rosie): Joshua, my love, thank you for your enduring and endless support. Your encouragement and uplifting spirit have given me the strength to continue in this journey. Your helping hand and words of confidence have meant more than I can ever express. Your faithful prayers have raised me up during this time. Mostly, your friendship has brought me deep gratitude. Your humor and out-of-the-blue jokes have given me the laughter and joy I have needed in the midst of this endeavor. I love you, babe! Your Rosie-girl!

Mama, without whom I could not have written this book, thank you for your prayers, encouragement, and great love. Looking back over the years of my illness, I cannot begin to pen my gratitude for all you did. Your constant care, sacrificing spirit, and loving arms brought me sustaining life and gave me the fuel to fight through. The promising verses you read provided me with renewed hope and faith each day. Your dedication to fight for me and with me showed a taste of God's constant protection and provision for us, His children. Since the years of the illness, the friendship we have developed has built me up and continues to inspire me. Our coffee dates and shopping adventures bring me a warm smile every time. I want to thank you, dear Mama, for all you have done and brought to my life. My deep love always!

Papa, you have my unending gratitude. Thank you for your words of promise fourteen years ago. They gave me the strength to keep fighting and the hope that we, our family, would make it through together. Your sacrifices to provide consistently for our family have shown me the tangibility of Christ. Through this process, I have felt your prayers as they spurred me on to keep on keeping on. Your words of, "Remember whose you are, a child of the Most High King," will echo through my mind for a lifetime. Thank you, Daddy. I love you dearly.

Jeremiah, my brother, your humor has been a source of true laughter and a soothing touch over the years, especially during the years of the illness. Thank you for your continual prayers, your encouraging spirit, and your strength. I love you!

Grandma Takacs, your dedication to prepare my food for those years helped keep me alive. The prayers of your church and friends contributed to my healing. Thank you for your sacrifices, your dedication, and your love.

Uncle Paul, thank you for your love and constant prayers over the years. Your recent telling of your favorite birthday was such a blessing to me. Emily, during my illness, your cards and letters brought me much-needed encouragement to hang on and fight through to see better days. The times of laughter and great adventure still bring a smile to my face. Much love and gratefulness, dear friend. Sami, your loyalty and ability to sit by my side all those years gave me a taste of God's abounding peace. Your love and companionship and your sweet and quiet words brought me great comfort. Thank you, my friend. Bethany, your constant prayers and uplifting words during this whole writing process mean more to me than I could begin to express. You are truly a God-given gift to me. Thank you, my friend. Janneke, my cherished friend, your jubilant spirit has brought me abounding joy and warmth over these years and months. Your deep love, caring heart, and words of tenacity have blessed me beyond compare. I love you, my sister in Christ. Stefanie, your quirky humor hits me every time with a smile and a laugh. Your thoughts and prayers have been greatly felt, and your excitement for this journey has ignited me to push through. I thank you, my loving friend. Tina, my friend, thank you for your prayers, support, and cheerful spirit over the years. To everyone at Family, thank you for your prayers and constant support.

Our thanks go out to Dr. Michael Ledtke, Mary Rose's medical doctor. Your work with Mary Rose throughout the years and your dedication to helping those with Lyme disease has helped us maintain our faith in God's healing process. Our deep appreciation goes out to Dr. Dale Flora. You have not only been an incredible help as our chiropractor, but your words of wisdom, shared on so many occasions, have also endeared you to us. Thanks for lending us your smile and wit when that's what we needed most! Cathy, Sherry, Judy, Sue, and Pat, thanks for being so patient in the scheduling process over the past twelve years!

The devotion to prayer of countless people has renewed our hope when we thought it may have run out. In the writing of this book, our lives have intersected with people who have influenced us for good and for God. Pastors Glenn Teal and Doug Langford, you were with us in the thick of things. Your presence, in many ways, brought us peace amidst the chaos and confusion. Thank you, Pastor Dean Angell, for the words of encouragement often given in your messages of the past two years. In the beginning of our writing process, you prayed for us and said God would use this book to heal. You were right; healing has come from the retelling of our experiences. Pastor

Tyson Nofzinger, your reflections and our conversations have helped point us in the right direction; many thanks. Our final thanks go out to those at WestBow Press who have helped us with putting our book together. Jeff Murray and Amanda Parsons, your kindness, ideas, and patience in answering our myriad of questions have made the process smoother and less intimidating.

To everyone and any we may have inadvertently overlooked, we love you, and you have our deep appreciation Thank you for the many ways you have been "Jesus with hands and feet" for our family during the difficult years with the illness or in the journey of this book.

Introduction

Springtime holds a keen awareness of new beginnings. After winter's enduring hibernation, the sights and smells of the coming season welcome new life. Flowers begin to bloom, trees fill with vibrant green leaves, and the air becomes warm. The permeating excitement traditionally felt at this time of year was lacking for our family in the spring of 1998.

Mary Rose, then turning ten years old, was not her usual self. Her persistent energy wasn't as abundant, her ability to concentrate was being severely hampered, and her digestive system was failing to function as it should. She complained of headaches that would not go away. Even her teachers commented on the changes in her schoolwork and usual stamina. It appeared she had an ongoing flu. Countless doctor's visits and medical tests yielded no answers. We were told it would only be a matter of time and she should feel better. It didn't appear, however, that time was a luxury we could afford.

Life as we knew it began to change drastically. After a nine-month search, the answer to the mysterious symptoms was found. Mary Rose was diagnosed with acute Lyme disease. The day we were given this news was a bittersweet one. I (Mary Rose) remember it like it was yesterday. As I lay on the doctor's examining table with my parents standing on either side of me, the doctor entered the room. He closed the door and took a tape recorder out of his lab coat pocket. He told us, "Things will get worse before they get better. But I will do my very best for her." I can remember thinking, *What could be worse?* That day my father carried me into the doctor's office because I was no longer able to walk. The thought of things becoming worse before they got better was overwhelming to me as a ten-year-old. Yet, the knowledge we were given gave me hope to know how best to fight.

For myself (Marianne), as the mother, the news received was as heartbreaking as it was welcomed. We finally had our answers, and I was thankful. But the implications for the future were terrifying. As we traveled the hour and a half trip back down from Royal Oak, Michigan, to our hometown of Temperance, we talked quietly about the news we had received. I watched my daughter in the seat next to me, trying gently to comfort her. She was in obvious pain, evidenced by her soft moaning. The ride home from the doctor's office was subdued as my husband and I met eyes in the rearview mirror. Our thoughts, revealed in our maintained eye contact, seemed to be on the same wavelength. *Now we know the truth we've been praying for, but what does that mean for our family?*

After arriving home, we found my mother-in-law and son waiting anxiously for us. As my husband settled our daughter into her hospital bed in the family room, I sat with our son to give him the sobering news. With heavy hearts, we then explained what the next couple of weeks would look like. Travel back and forth to the doctor's office for further tests and consultations would be commonplace, the staff had informed us before we left. My mother-in-law assured us she and my father-in-law would be there for us and would do whatever it took to help the family through this difficult time. Having the assurance we would not be alone gave us encouragement. The belief that God was also with us gave us hope as we prayed for the days ahead.

This was the beginning of a five-year time frame in which there were many ups and downs to fighting an illness that turned from acute to chronic. Our family faced many challenges as we learned a new way of life. Medicines would come and go, and experimental regimens would be tried. Mary Rose took steps forward and backward.

All the while, as a family we were trying to be brave in supporting one another. We discovered our energies physically, mentally, and spiritually were being severely taxed. It became clear we would need to learn how to reach out to others for help. The new doctor Mary Rose began seeing in the fall of 1998 stated it well when he said we would be shaken to the core of our faith. He was right. The inner struggles we faced with ongoing stress, fatigue, and a roller coaster of emotions drove us to our knees. It was with this journey in mind that we began writing this book nearly a year ago.

It was after my (Mary Rose's) college graduation in May of 2010 that Mom and I began seriously talking about co-authoring a book. We had often tossed around the idea of writing or perhaps speaking about the struggles we faced and the answers God provided. People frequently commented on the bond between us. It was not uncommon for Mom and I to talk with others about God's incredible faithfulness and healing power. Still, the thought of writing a book seemed intimidating, and the timing was never right, until last July.

As we began this devotional last summer, both Mary Rose and I knew we were going to be sharing our stories of significant struggles as well as how we overcame them with God. Frequently our challenges brought us to places of waiting and taught us how to patiently endure. Each circumstance we encountered taught us lessons about ourselves and about God, ones we remember today. As you read through this thirty-day devotional, we encourage you to find a quiet spot where you can clearly sense God speaking to your heart. He may show you how humor is critical to lift your spirit in the midst of life's difficulties. Perhaps, like us, you have some things to let go of and others to embrace.

Depending on your particular situation, the order in which you read the devotions may vary from how we have them laid out. In order to avoid confusion, we have placed our individual names directly under the title of each day to distinguish which of us authored the day. There is no sequence or chronological order to the days. No matter where you find yourself today, our hope for you is that you will sense, through the stories we've shared, that *you are not alone*. We pray God will bless you with encouragement that uplifts, faith that is strengthened, and a peace that surpasses all understanding. Last, our hope is that you gain an awareness that God has not abandoned you to your circumstances and in fact, is carrying you in the palm of His hand.

Blessings to you,

Marianne and Mary Rose

~ 1 ~

The Choices We Make
Marianne

The Lord is close to the brokenhearted and saves those who are
crushed in spirit.
—Psalm 34:18

The cry of my daughter's heart was audible as she asked "Mommy,
what did I do to deserve this?" How do you explain to your child
that she isn't to blame for being sick? She didn't do anything that
could precipitate a catastrophic illness. At the age of ten, and in
tremendous pain, my daughter pled for an answer. She wanted
to know what she had done wrong so she could try never to do it
again. Does that sound familiar? How many times do we ask God
what we did to deserve something? We find it hard to understand
the truth. God doesn't make people sick or cause things we tend to
blame Him for. He is, however, faithful to be there with us through
the circumstances we face.

Quietly, gently, so as not to disturb the bed she lay in, I sat next to
my daughter. I knew the slightest movement could cause her physical
pain to increase. Trying to steady my breaking heart, I looked into
her eyes, which were rimmed with tears, and knew it was a moment
of truth for both of us. I tried to explain, to bring comprehension
and truth to her thinking that God was not the cause of what she was
going through. It's not His character. "Further," I heard myself say
aloud as I prayed silently, "I don't know why you are sick. We may
never know the why of this." My thoughts continued to tumble out.

1

"But there are some things we do know, and we are going to choose to believe those truths." There were no words to make the pain go away or to change the circumstances of the moment, only truth that could change our way of viewing things. I let my daughter ask what she needed to, without fear of the possible answers.

God is faithful; of this I had been sure. I had seen His faithfulness in my life and in the lives of others around me. After all, hadn't He been faithful in providing someone to help point us in the right direction to get an accurate diagnosis of my daughter's health? Hadn't He also answered the specific prayer I prayed to ask that we find out the truth of what was happening to her, no matter what the truth was? Although I was scared about what the future held, I had to make a choice. "We are going to hold God to His word and believe He is faithful," were the words I spoke to my daughter and the truth I chose to believe. She looked at me and nodded, trusting I was telling her the truth.

As we sat together on that afternoon, now so long ago, our hearts were being comforted. A peace settled in my soul. I knew I could rest in the fact that God would be there with us, and no matter what we were to face, we wouldn't do it alone. The words of Jesus, found in John, chapter 14, were coming alive to me. I was realizing that the same counselor, the "Spirit of truth" that Jesus had asked His father to provide for His disciples, was right there with me and my family. Little did I know how much I would rely on the truth of those words to carry me through the months and years yet to come. As Mary Rose and I searched the scriptures together, we came across the promise in Psalm 34:18: "The Lord is close to the brokenhearted and saves those who are crushed in spirit." These were words that described us both and would be read over and over again as we continued to face the future. Mary Rose found particular comfort in hearing Psalm 23 read to her. We talked about Jesus being our shepherd and how we could imagine walking with Him beside quiet waters, as the psalm describes. We were learning that, although things around us were uncertain and could be terrifying, we would find peace within us as we chose to focus on God and His promises.

Truth in Action

What is your moment of truth? Have you received devastating news about health issues, a job, or infidelity? Life can be seemingly calm one moment and change dramatically with a single phone call or letter. Such was the case of our family. As our world changed beyond our control, it was difficult to believe that God was still with us. Choices had to be made. When facing those moments of great uncertainty, don't be afraid to be honest and raw with God. We are told throughout the Bible that God will be with us. He is described as our refuge and strength, an ever-present help in troubled times. We are told in Joshua 1:9 not to be afraid, but rather strong and courageous, because our God is with us. Our fears can be paralyzing. If we give in to the fears, then the already-difficult circumstances will seem insurmountable. So like my daughter and myself, you may need to make a choice to believe that God is faithful. He will give you aid, and He has not abandoned you, even in the moments when it does not appear to be the case. When you face your moment of truth, know that as God's child, you do so with His promise for shelter, help, and refuge. Read through the verses mentioned here today. You will soon discover many promises, made by a loving God, for those who choose to follow Him. Cling to the truths about His character, and watch as those truths soothe your pain and begin to renew your hope.

Reflection/Journal

_____
_____
_____
_____
_____
_____
_____
_____
_____
_____
_____
_____
_____
_____
_____
_____
_____
_____
_____
_____
_____
_____
_____
_____
_____
_____
_____
_____
_____

~ 2 ~

The Ripple Effect
Mary Rose

A man of many companions may come to ruin, but there is a
friend who sticks closer than a brother.
—Proverbs 18:24

I am not sure how to start this story, what to say in the opening
paragraph, or how to capture you to keep you reading on. If you
can bear with me for a moment, you will soon understand why. This
story will be similar to a roller coaster ride. I don't know the speed
at which it will go, the height it will climb, or the dips it will take,
but I do know the ending. I know where the ride will lead, and if
you can sit back and take it in, it will be worth the trip.

It was Christmas of 2001, Christmas Eve, to be exact. I can
remember it as if it was yesterday. It was a turning point; the light
at the end of the tunnel was coming closer, and Christmas Eve was
the highlight.

Throughout my illness, my family tried to keep our holiday
traditions alive, and Christmas Eve was one of them. Our family
and another family we are close with celebrate every December
24th together. We first go to our Christmas Eve church services
and then gather at one of our homes to share the holiday meal and
evening together. This is a tradition we've held for fourteen years
and counting.

As we sit around the table to eat our traditional Christmas Eve
meal, Chinese food, we talk about what we have faced over the year,

what we have learned, and what we hope for in the coming year. It's a beautiful time of laughter, love, and fellowship. After dinner, we have the wonderful tradition of watching one of the greatest Christmas movies ever made. You guessed it—*National Lampoon's Christmas Vacation*. Yes, we spend time with the Griswolds on the Eve of Christmas. There is much laughter, great lines shared, and a joy that fills the home we are meeting in. As you can tell, I love our families' Christmas Eve tradition, and for Christmas Eve 2001, I loved it all the more.

We gathered at our house that year, after the Christmas Eve service. The food had been placed on the table, and everyone began to gather around. I was to join them, but I waited several feet away in my wheelchair until everyone was seated. My mom's friend Leslie looked over at me as if to say, "Isn't Rosie going to join us?" As everyone sat, waiting for me, I began to lift myself from my chair and stand. Slowly, with one foot in front of the other, I walked to the table. Leslie's eyes were wide and filled with tears as she leapt from her chair to hug me tightly. It was a miracle! I was walking— something that, nearly six weeks prior, my physical therapist told me I would never do again. I had not been able to walk for two years.

The rest of the evening was filled with great joy and celebration as our friends reminisced over the countless prayers they had prayed that were now being answered right before their eyes. They were visibly encouraged to see God's tangible answer. I can still, to this day, see and hear in my mind the joy and laughter of that Christmas Eve. It is one I hold very dear to my heart, but for different reasons than you may think. I wanted nothing more than for our friends to be the first family, outside of my own and my doctors, to share in the celebration, and they were. For me, that evening was about celebrating how God had answered their prayers and sharing in the joy and hope it brought them.

This family was one of the families that remained close to us in the midst of my illness. We remain good friends to this day. They were part of the few that stood in the gap for my family and me during my illness. They prayed constantly and faithfully for us. Despite our pain, hurt, turmoil, and doubt, they stood by us, even in their own doubt. God gave them the ability to do these things, to be Jesus in the flesh for us. They stood in the middle of our storm, reaching out to us, to give us hope.

Although I know that God gave them the ability to stand in the gap for our family, I recognize that they chose to allow God to use them in this way. For that blessing, I am forever grateful. Yet I can almost guarantee that if you were to ask them how they did this, they would give you two answers. First, they would give all the glory to God for the ways they were able to help us. Second, they would say that by watching us go through what we did, it encouraged and grew their faith more.

The truth is, most of the time, our circumstances affect those around us. It's the ripple effect, just like when a raindrop hits a puddle of water. It can affect those around us in good and bad ways. Often, when we're facing incredibly trying times, our faith is stretched and grows as a result. This happens usually for two reasons. The first being it takes us to our knees before Christ for our loved one. It is in this time we tend to ask God to save, comfort, direct, and love them and to show us how best to be there for them.

The second reason is simple. Just as they are facing their situation, it is likely we may be facing one of our own. Truth be told, it can be comforting to know that others are in, or have faced previously, challenges similar to ours—not because we want others to be going through the trenches as well, but because it always helps to know we are neither alone, nor the only ones facing hardship. Each of us needs to know that Christ is carrying us through and that He will put people in our lives to help us by standing in the gap.

Truth in Action

I don't know where you find yourself today, what you're facing, the demons you're fighting, or the road you're on, but I do know God wants you to be blessed by someone. He wants you to see that someone—a sister, a brother, your mother or father, a friend or even a coworker—is standing in the gap for you. You might be asking what it means to stand in the gap for someone, or better yet, what this looks like. It's someone God gives great love for you—someone who prays for you, encourages you to keep fighting, and helps you to laugh along the way. That person may know they are this for you or they may not, because they may understand what it means or they may not. Ultimately, that doesn't matter as much. What matters is that God has chosen that person to be there for you, and they are choosing to do the things God is asking of them.

Our friends, with whom we still spend every Christmas Eve, were some of the people who stood in the gap for us. I know God gave them deep love for our family, and out of that love came the tools to help us. So I ask you today, who is it that is standing in the gap for you? Who is it that is praying for you? Who are those people that are giving you encouragement, strength, and hope to keep on keeping on? Who is God using to fuel your tank?

If you are going through the midst of something and know who is standing in the gap for you, thank that person. If you are on the other side and can look back and see who God gave you during that time or perhaps who you still have, go and share how deeply their love and aid meant to you. Now, if you do not have someone like this, ask God to bring that person into your life, and hold tight to His promise that He will. It says in Psalm 18:6, "In my distress I called to the Lord; I cried to my God for help. From his temple he heard my voice; my cry came before him, into his ears," so may you rest assured that when you cry out to God, He hears you and He will answer your plea.

Reflection/Journal

_____
_____
_____
_____
_____
_____
_____
_____
_____
_____
_____
_____
_____
_____
_____
_____
_____
_____
_____
_____
_____
_____
_____
_____
_____
_____
_____
_____
_____
_____
_____

~ 3 ~

Learning to Serve
Marianne

Whatever you do, work at it with all your heart, as working for the
Lord, not for men.
—Colossians 3:23

Minutes turned into hours, and hours became days. Days were
giving way to seasons. The ever-present question circled in my
mind. *Lord*, I pled in my mind, *what is going on?* It seemed
for every little bit of progress, time was endless. I watched my
daughter struggle to eat as she took a bite of food once every
ten minutes. Each meal lasted approximately one to two hours,
making for a sum total of about five to six hours a day for meal
times. Digestive problems, due to her illness, caused food to
virtually fly through my daughter's system. Very little nutrition
was able to be absorbed. Weakening muscles meant she needed
to have someone feed her.

I reflected back to some months previous. Doctors were baffled as
they tried, unsuccessfully, to watch the nonexistent nutritional path
of my daughter's digestive tract. As quickly as food was swallowed,
a seemingly mysterious force pulled it straight down and out of
her body. She was receiving no nutrition from her food intake.
X-rays could not be captured because of the swiftness of the exiting
food. It was suggested we would need to feed her small bites every
few minutes in hopes that some nutrition would stay with her. *No*

kidding, I thought to myself. That much we had already determined. No other answers were forthcoming.

As I sat in the quiet of our home feeding my daughter, I mentally revisited the roads we had traveled. We spent much time experimenting with various foods in hopes something would settle in her stomach. Through a tedious process of elimination, we narrowed her food choices down to the one thing she could eat: plain organic oatmeal. This had been her source of sustenance, three times a day, for about four to six months. Recently, however, Mary Rose was able to tolerate my mother-in-law's chicken noodle soup. She could tolerate it in the sense that she was able to keep it down when nothing else would stay, besides oatmeal.

I was grateful for the faithfulness of my in-laws. Mom Takacs, upon discovering the good news, set about to make pots and pots of chicken noodle soup to can. Dad Takacs would make delivery of the soup to our home from thirty minutes away. I marveled at their dedication and patience. Mary Rose was no longer limited to eating only one food, thanks to her grandparents. It dawned on me at about that time that progress was being made. Granted, it wasn't coming as quickly as we would have preferred, but it was coming. My daughter now had two foods to eat, and soon, a third would be introduced to her diet.

As I leaned over to give my daughter another bite of food, I felt a stirring in my heart. An answer was forthcoming—an answer to my query of what was happening. The Lord gently pointed out the service of my in-laws and of many around us. God helped me realize that as we continued to walk the long and tedious journey, we were learning to become better servants for Him, even as we watched the service of those around us. The gentle prodding came to me, "Whatever you do, do it for Me, because it's Me you're serving." I recalled having read similar words in the bible, from Colossians 3:23. Paul reminds the church, "Whatever you do, work at it with all your heart, as working for the Lord, not for men." My mind reverted back to the task at hand, and I smiled at my daughter as tears came to my eyes. I found myself feeling very thankful to be at my daughter's side. I knew I would learn to persevere, just as James had said in James

1:12, "Blessed is a man who perseveres under trial, for once he has been approved, he will receive the crown of life, which the Lord has promised to those who love Him."

Truth in Action

Are you facing a long period of suffering? Does it appear, despite your best efforts, that progress isn't coming quickly enough in your circumstances? With the knowledge you are truly doing your very best and are following a carefully chosen path for recovery, ask God to give you perseverance so you can keep going. You may not see the circumstances around you change all that quickly, but you will witness a transformation in your own outlook. You may need to learn to rest in God. Paul tells us in Hebrew 4:9-10, "There remains then a Sabbath-rest for the people of God. For anyone who enters God's rest, also rests from his works, just as God did from his." My challenge for you, then, is to learn to leave things in God's hands, for His timing. Ask God to show you how to rest in Him while you persevere in your circumstances. For some this will be very difficult, but that's okay. God won't throw His hands in the air and wonder what He needs to do next. He won't punish you for having a hard time. Those are not the ways of a loving God or father. He *will* let you know, however, that He can take care of things. He knows the broader picture and the essence of time.

Your circumstances could be very different from mine. Perhaps you are waiting for a positive change to be headed your way and it doesn't appear to be near coming. Maybe you wonder if what you are doing even matters. It does. God sees everything we do. He knows our thoughts even before we think them. Jesus understands what it means to want a different path, yet knowing it is not going to change. When He knelt one last time to pray in the Garden of Gethsemane on the night before His crucifixion, He asked for a different road. He prayed in anguish. In His heart, though, was purpose. He knew His death was imminent. His service to us to bring salvation wasn't yet finished. Only the heart of a loving servant could face what He willingly faced for us. When the road seems unbearably long and you can't see an end, ask Jesus to ignite in you a servant's desire and grace you with perseverance for the road ahead. Ask Him to help you see the broader picture, the one only He can see. He will give you a heart of gratitude and the ability to cope beyond the here and now of your circumstances.

Reflection/Journal

- 4 -

What You Need from a Friend
Mary Rose

He makes me lie down in green pastures, He leads me beside quite
waters, He restores my soul.
—Psalm 32:2

No matter what we are facing in life, whether it is a difficult
and painful situation or a time of great joy and blessing, we all need
friends who will stand by our side through the thick and the thin
and laugh with us in the in-between. Our friends provide us with
different yet needed qualities. Some provide laughter, some comfort,
some encouragement, and some strength. Yet, in the midst of this
handful of friends, we all thirst for one or two who are more than
just a friend, those who stand out among the rest. They're not blood
family, but they're just as much like family to us. It's in the difficult
circumstance of our lives that we long for these few to surround us
and lift us up. We may not know what we need from our friend,
but we know we need something, and many times it's simply their
presence.

During my illness, I faced one of those times. What I desperately
needed was a friend who would stick by me no matter what the
situation brought. By God's watchful and loving eye, He provided
me with such a friend. I had a handful or so of friends who were
with me throughout my illness. This friend in particular sat by my
side unlike any other. She hung in there with me through the best
and the worst of it all. Even when things were at there worst and I

15

had no words to speak, no thoughts to think, and no energy to give to anyone, my friend Sami was there.

She, at the age of eight, and through her early teen years, would come over and just be with me. We didn't need to talk, we didn't need to play a game, and we didn't even need to watch something on TV. Sami would just sit there and stay with me. I found such comfort in those moments. Despite the anguish I was feeling and the anger over the situation I had, she cared enough to put her life on hold for those moments in time and just *be* with me. It astounds me to this day that God blessed me with such a friend as she was. At that point in time, I could not walk, I could not feed myself, and I could not lift my body into my wheelchair. Sami was not bothered by my inability to give back. She accepted me as I was. She was willing to sit there and allow her presence and the silence to bring me comfort.

Looking back at that time, I can honestly say my friend probably did not know what her presence did for me. Truth be told, at that time, I did not understand what her being there provided for me. I just knew it made me feel very, very loved. Her care and kindness provided a soothing to my soul. I would imagine she didn't know what to say or do but figured at least if she was there, it might provide me with something, and it certainly did.

Thinking back on this time, now nearly thirteen years later, I do not know how my friend stayed by my side at such a young age. Looking at children of that age as a twenty-two-year-old now, I do not know if many eight-year-olds would sit for hours in silence with their ill friend. Perhaps some would, but most would not. Honestly, I don't know if I would have had the courage and strength to stay with one of my friends as my friend stayed with me. Coming to that realization over the years has led me to see God's hand in it all. Christ was not only my personal friend, the one I talked to about any and everything, but He was also the one who reached out to me through Sami. She allowed Him to be her hands and feet, and because of this, she was not only the friend I needed, but so was Christ.

Truth in Action

Are you in need of a friend who sticks closer than a brother? God promises us in Proverbs 18:24 that this is possible. In the middle of our whirlwind, there can be and will be a friend who stands by your side. Christ Himself will be that friend. If you let Him, He will show Himself to you in a way you cannot even imagine possible. He will become your love, your confidante, your most-trusted advisor, and the one who heals your heart, soothes your soul, and brings health to your body. If you do not know Christ as such a friend, ask Him to become this for you. If do know Jesus as this but your heart is longing for a friend, ask Christ to bring this person alongside of you. He will. Christ Himself needed not only His relationship with His Father but also relationships with His twelve closest friends.

If you are one who has a friend or family member going through a difficult time, I challenge you to come alongside that person. Sit with your loved one, cry with him or her, and laugh with him or her. Pray and ask God to show you what that person needs. Perhaps an encouraging word, a good laugh, a quiet moment, or to cry a painful tear with him or her is all that is needed. Remember, you need not be afraid to trust God. He will use you to provide whatever your loved one needs. You're the vessel; He's the captain. Allow God to put into practice your ability to "be." It's those quiet moments that are soothing to the soul like cool aloe to a fresh burn. They provide the renewing of our hope. Last but not least, no matter what situation you find yourself in today, do not be afraid to "be" with God. Psalm 62:5 tells us, "Find rest, O my soul, in God alone; my hope comes from him." In this place, we find rest and a new strength. As my friend could be with me, I, too, can be with God, and oh how soothing is He.

Reflection/Journal

~ 5 ~

Called to Comfort
Marianne

Praise be to the God and Father of our Lord Jesus Christ, the
Father of compassion and the God of all comfort, who comforts
us in all our troubles, so that we can comfort those in any trouble
with the comfort we ourselves received from God.
—2 Corinthians 3:3-4

On one particularly difficult day, I was struggling with what sense I
could make of the circumstances of my daughter's illness. My friend
Carleen and I were talking on the phone. Sensing my discouragement,
she was careful to listen more than speak. She didn't offer clichés or
try to find the perfect thing to say that would seemingly make it all
better. She knew better than to even try.

Our friendship had begun at a book sale being held in my
daughter's honor. Carleen had experienced the devastation of an
illness through a parent's eyes, just as I was doing. She was all too
familiar with the heartache of watching while disease ravages your
child's body. Pouring out my heart on the phone with her, I shared
how the future appeared to be very dark and murky to me. Carleen
was able to steer my thoughts to a calmer place, just as a rudder steers
for a boat. She carefully weighed her words before she spoke in reply
to my mother's cry. Although the present days were excruciatingly
painful to experience and clarity difficult to find, a better day would
come, Carleen encouraged. Her words rang true. In the fashion of
a realist, Carleen did not deny the pain of the moment, but neither

did she ignore the truth that change would eventually come. She knew things would make some sense in time. For some, those words may sound trite. I apologize if that is the case. Knowing the place they came from in Carleen's heart, I sensed there was a knowing. Further, she predicted a day would come when I would share with someone else the life-affirming words she blessed me with. She was right on both counts.

I suspect Carleen had no idea she was used of God that day. In 1 Corinthians 1:3-4, we are told God comforts us with the comfort we will one day share with someone else. Carleen was the comfort of God for me through the words of our conversation. I was starting to learn that although life could be painful and terribly unfair, God was still good. He is always the same, no matter how hard the storms of life are beating us down. It was becoming clear to me the truth of Paul's words, found in 2 Corinthians 4:8, "We are hard pressed on every side, but not crushed; perplexed, but not in despair; persecuted but not abandoned; struck down, but not destroyed." It was a matter of perspective.

Although the circumstances of our lives did not begin to turn for the better for quite a while, I knew I had support from people around me. At times I made the call for help to someone. At other times, people reached out to give comfort through their words, with a hug, or in serving our family otherwise. No matter the way, it all came with the same message, "We're here for you." This made the days and months ahead easier to go through until the corner would be turned for the better.

Truth In Action

If you are in need of comfort today, sit in a quiet place and listen. Take a walk, if you prefer, and pay attention to how God might be speaking to your heart in the surroundings. At times, it's the gentle breeze you feel on your face that lets you know God is there, listening, and letting you feel the brush of His hand. Other times the serenity of watching the waves rolling up to the shoreline gives a sense of the incredible constancy of God and the peace only He can bestow. Open your Bible and read. Ask Him to show you comfort in His love letter to you. Check out 1 Corinthians 1:3-4 for yourself. If you let Him, God can show you comfort in the form of another human being. When you need a human touch, don't be afraid to dial that cell phone! There are people just waiting in the proverbial wings to get the call from you. They are waiting, praying for you, and hoping you will let them comfort you. If you know someone in the midst of trial, you can be the comfort of God to that friend. Paul reminds us in Galatians 6:2 to carry one another's burdens. Comfort will look different depending on the person's needs at the time: a listening ear, a heartfelt hug, words of compassion, or a meal prepared all speak the presence of God. They are love in the tangible form of comfort. Pray before you speak or act. Ask God to show you how to reach out. He loves an open heart and willingly gives guidance. If we search God's Word, He continually reminds us He is an ever-present help and hope in troubled times. Read through the Psalms. You will find a familiar pattern in many of them. Oftentimes a cry for help goes out. Frustration, fear, or anger are then expressed toward someone. A song of trust and rejoicing in God generally ends the same psalm. My prayer for you is that you will be able to say with David in Psalm 62, "My soul rests in God alone, He is my rock, and in Him I will find refuge."

Reflection/Journal

~ 6 ~

Laughter Soothes
Mary Rose

He will yet fill your mouth with laughter and your lips with shouts of joy.
—Job 8:21

How many times do the gospels depict Jesus rejoicing with the little children, with His disciples, and with His family? The truth is even Christ Himself needed to rejoice in His life, and a big part of rejoicing is having laughter. Christ needed laughter to provide humor, to bring joy, and to even soothe His soul. If He needed laughter, how much more do we? Throughout my illness, nothing soothed my soul like laughter. I had many times of sorrow, discomfort, and pain, but when laughter came, it renewed my spirit like the sun's illumination after a hard rainstorm.

At the age of twelve, my body began making strides toward better health and healing. Shortly after, at age thirteen, I went with my friends from youth group to a youth camp retreat. At this time, I was still in my wheelchair, as I was unable to walk any lengthy distances. I can remember the experience plain as day. My friend was pushing me up a hill and joking around about how fun it would be if once reaching the top, she let me go. I wasn't too keen on the idea since I would be traveling downhill without someone steering or holding on to my wheelchair. Needless to say, upon reaching the top, my friend took her hands off my chair, and there I went racing down the hill. The hill was actually a road, with a car on it heading my way. Neither of us saw the car at first because it had just pulled out from a side street.

You can probably imagine my fear as I was heading toward the oncoming car. At that point my friend, still oblivious to the car, was laughing as she heard me yell and wave my arms about. The problem was, I wasn't yelling at her; I was yelling *to her* about the oncoming car. Once she realized this and saw the car, she bolted down the hill and quickly grabbed my wheelchair. Jerking it to the right, we both went tumbling into the grass. As we landed in the soft grass, we began laughing hysterically! The fear of colliding with the car and the brief frustration I had with her for letting go of me existed no more. Laughter was all that escaped our mouths! It was one of those freaky situations you never think you will find yourself in, but when you do, all you can do is laugh about it. Of course, I have given her a hard time about it over the years! Even to this day when it's brought into a conversation, we will both look at each other and start laughing!

For myself, that is a memory I smile at because the trip was bittersweet for me. I had worked very hard health-wise in order to go, but I still wasn't able to be there without being in my wheelchair. That fact proved to be frustrating for me. I was tired of not living a normal life like my friends, and I wanted so badly to feel normal. Even though the ability to go brought me joy and great encouragement, God knew what I needed more was laughter—real, hurts the stomach and can't breathe laughter, the very thing He provided through my friend and her brilliant idea. He also knew what the outcome would be, and safety was not the issue.

It was in this time and many others throughout my illness when I felt the humorous side of Christ. It's when I learned all the more that He created laughter and loves when we laugh, not just in the good times. I personally believe He takes even greater joy when we can laugh in the midst of life's difficulties. It is in the difficult times that the enemy tries to steal our joy and laughter away. Unfortunately for us, so much of the time we allow it. It is in the trials of life when God wants nothing more than for His children to find joy in Him. He understands how laughter brings us healing. This kind of healing is vitally important to our ability to keep pressing on. The truth is, in the midst of the painful times of life, laughter is one of the best antidotes for our hearts and spirits.

Truth in Action

Do you find yourself in a circumstance where every turn you take leads to another part of the maze, and frustration has hit the boiling point? If this is you, ask God to provide you with laughter. Sometimes the laughter will come from a bizarre and unexpected situation, similar to mine, where all you can do is laugh about it. Other times, laughter may come from a joke someone says, a random word your child utters, or a situation that is purely humorous. God wants you to have the joy of laughter. He wants you to rejoice in Him no matter the circumstance. Philippians 4:4 promises, "Rejoice in the Lord always. I will say it again Rejoice!" This is not always an easy thing to accomplish, but Christ will provide you with a reason to laugh and rejoice. God will bring humor, and He will give us the gift of His joy within it. So in the midst of life's trials, when something crazy and unexpected happens that leaves you in a fit of laughter, accept this for what it is: a gift from your heavenly Father!

Reflection/Journal

~ 7 ~

Remember His Benefits
Marianne

Praise the Lord, O my soul, and forget not all His benefits.
—Psalm 103:2

"*Brrrr*, the air sure is cold for Halloween night," I complained to myself as we made our way to our friend's home for dinner. Mary Rose had taken a turn for the better. We were in a state of cautious celebration. It was getting colder earlier than normal for southeast Michigan. The cold weather outside was of little consequence compared to the warmth of being with friends who were like family. It made for a toasty warm fire in the heart.

As we pulled into the driveway, we prepared for the routine of getting out the wheelchair with its various parts and pieces my daughter needed. It was a familiar pattern by now, as we had been using the wheelchair for a while. But what was new territory was the feeling of normalcy. This was one of the firsts for us. After many months of being confined to her home, my daughter was well enough to go to our friend's home for the holiday. Our friends had been looking forward to the occasion as much as we were. It didn't matter that Mary Rose yet depended on the wheelchair for transportation. Our hearts were overjoyed to see her expressions and laughter as we entered our friend's home.

Recent months had brought with it many steps forward, at last! We were optimistic as we prepared to start the upcoming holiday season. I was feeling incredibly thankful, yet my heart was not totally at peace. I wondered what I was fussing over. It seemed, in light of recent positive steps forward, I should be feeling more peaceful. Uncertain as to what the confusion in my heart was about, I asked the Lord to show me what was going on internally. Despite my seeming willingness to discover an answer, I wasn't getting a sense of what was causing my inner unrest. Hmm, I guess I just needed to let it go for now; back to the moment at hand.

A meal shared with those closest to us seemed to lift my spirits. I observed as we ate dinner, and I was happy to see the smiling faces of our friends and their children. They made every effort to include Mary Rose in the celebration as costumes were donned for the evening's festivities. We bundled up, blanketed our daughter, and headed out to the neighborhood. My friend and I talked about our fond memories of trick-or-treating as children. We *ooh*ed and *awwe*d at the creativity displayed in the costumes of the kids who sprawled the neighborhood. My friend's boys and our son joined up with us momentarily as we made the rounds. I watched them run off to gather more candy. I was content with life but was wishing Mary Rose could run around with the rest of the kids. I had my daughter by my side. We were doing life normally, as we had longed for. What did I have to be sad about? As we walked around farther, I laughed at the silliness of my husband joking with our daughter. Yep, life was good. But what was that nagging feeling in my heart? I needed to think about this further another time. For the moment, I was immersed in the laughter and joy of the evening.

Within days of that Halloween celebration, I found myself crying in our bathroom. "Lord, please help me understand what is happening," I begged. As I thought back to Halloween night, I realized something. Joy wasn't the only emotion present that night. A whole host of other feelings were swarming my soul, threatening the joy I had experienced. It was time to do a little soul searching. One by one, the Lord would take me through the other thoughts and feelings I was ignoring.

Despite the feeling of joy at watching my daughter participate in a holiday, without much worry of germs around us, my heart was saddened. As the other children ran around the streets, including my son, I was keenly aware my daughter might never walk, let alone run, the streets for Halloween. It pierced my heart. I wanted so very much to see her get out of the wheelchair and be able to do what the other kids could do. It was then that I realized how very ungrateful I was sounding, or so I thought. As I wrote my thoughts and confessed them openly to the Lord, I began to hear His gentle prodding deep within: "I love her more than you do, Marianne. You gave her to Me. When did you stop trusting Me with her? Give Me your concerns. Worrying about the future won't make things better or give you any peace."

Jesus reminded me of something I had heard long ago but was presently having a hard time keeping in mind. God didn't want me to worry. His word asks us in Matthew 6:27, which of us can add a single hour to our lives by worrying? The truth of the thoughts echoed in my mind. I cried, feeling remorseful that I was trying to play god. I wanted things to be as I thought best. Repentance of my lack of trust, my ungratefulness, and my fears soon followed. A gentle peace coaxed me to some favorite Scripture passages. The Lord brought to my mind, as He so frequently had, that He was with me. He was an ever-present help in trouble (Ps. 46:1). I saw with a new understanding how God had brought us to the place we were. Able to trust again, my heart felt lighter. No longer weighed by sadness, I could let God work in His own time.

Truth in Action

We are often reminded in Scripture to not forget God's benefits. Psalm 103:1-3 reminds us of some very important steps we need to take when we are in ongoing circumstances or seasons of life. First, it tells us to praise Him with our souls and with all that is within us. Why do we need to praise God? Because as we let ourselves acknowledge that God is good, faithful, and trustworthy, our hearts become convinced of these truth about Him. When our hearts are convinced, our words, our actions, and our lives are changed for the better—always for the better. Next, we are admonished to forget not His benefits. Sometimes when we are in a season that doesn't appear to be changing soon, we can forget the beauty of previous seasons. We need to look back, to remember the good God has brought to our lives. When we can do this, even just a little, it will encourage us for the present. We become less focused on the future and the what-ifs or if only. Last, the verses encourage us to remember that Jesus has forgiven all our sins, even our lack of trust and ungrateful hearts, and will heal all our diseases. The healing of a disease may not come here on earth, as we so desperately desire. As a friend recently reminded me, maybe not here, maybe only when we are finally face to face with Him, there will come a time when there will be no more tears and no more sickness, only the never-ending joy of being in God's presence. Whether you are facing a trying time or know someone who is, spend time thinking on God's benefits in your life. You'll soon find yourself in a better place within your heart.

As you take time to remember the benefits God has brought to you, take a few moments to look over Matthew 6:27 and Psalm 46:1, and pay attention to the surrounding text of each of these verses. You may notice in the contexts of what is written there is not a denying that trouble beckons at the door, wanting to enter in and bring with it worry and discouragement. God tells us, however, we will not be able to add years to our lives through worry. His assurance is that He is in control and is capable of carrying us through. He will be the one to work out the details, and He will bring us up out of our concerns if we let Him have them. Notice how Jesus wants us to be aware that worry will not add so much as an hour to our lives! In fact, as we are so often told today, worry *can* do the opposite, take away from our lives. Worry causes us needless stress and does nothing to resolve issues. It certainly doesn't grant any measure of peace, in my own personal experience. On the other hand, if we choose to trust God, what we can count on, as expressed in Psalm 46:1, is finding a refuge and strength in Him. Further, the Psalm reminds us He is with us always in troubled times. One of the most revealing verses in the Bible is when God says in Psalm 46:10, "Be still, and know that I am God." He waits for us to come before Him and be still. We need to be concerned about letting ourselves be quiet before Him in the midst of the storms of life. He will take care of all the rest.

Reflection/Journal

_____

_____

_____

_____

_____

_____

_____

_____

_____

_____

_____

_____

_____

_____

_____

_____

_____

_____

_____

_____

_____

_____

_____

_____

_____

_____

_____

_____

_____

~ 8 ~

Calming the Storm Within
Mary Rose

Then Peter got down out of the boat, walked on the water and
came toward Jesus. But when he saw the wind, he was afraid and,
beginning to sink, cried out, "Lord, save me!" Immediately Jesus
reached out his hand and caught him. "You of little faith," He
said, "why did you doubt?"
—Matthew 14:29-31

Every one of us faces points in our lives where we doubt God and
stop living by faith. We become fearful as we hear the wind howling
and see the storm approaching, and suddenly we begin to question
if God is really with us. Is He hearing our prayers? Does He know
the pain and the fear we are facing? Sometimes we even question,
does God really care, and does He truly love me? If He does, why
is He allowing this to happen in my life? If this is you today feeling
desperate, fearful, and doubting God, I say to you do not give up,
and please read on.

Over the years, I myself have faced the emotional and spiritual
storms of fear. It is a fear that paralyzes and a fear that can define
the outcome. At the age of eleven, I came to know this fear. Along
with the fear, doubt flooded in. I then began to stop trusting God
and living by faith. During that time, I feared for my life. I could
no longer walk, and my body was slowly withering away. I weighed
only sixty-seven pounds at the time. The disease had destroyed so

much of my digestive system that it hindered my body's ability to absorb nutrition.

I knew during those days, weeks, and months I needed to keep my eyes focused upon Christ, but I struggled every minute. I thought I needed to see God's physical presence, but I couldn't. Instead, all I could see was the storm circling around me. It was difficult to trust that God was with me, especially since He was not visible to me. As the situation grew worse, the fear of being alone and the fear of the unknown captured me. I began to take my eyes off Christ and place them on the storm. This led me to sink emotionally and spiritually, just like Peter during the storm at sea.

At that time, I had to distinguish between what I believed in my heart and what I thought in my mind. As I did this, I began to realize that even though I had little control over my body physically, I did have control over what I believed to be true. It was by this that I realized I did believe Christ was with me. As I prayed and trusted God, He gave me strength to keep fighting spiritually and emotionally. For me, coming to this understanding was Christ calming the storm within me. I think Peter, in Matthew 14:27-31, is the perfect example of our humanity in life's difficult circumstances. Peter is asked to take a step of faith, but he, like us, loses his footing when fear creeps in. Yet despite this, Christ still reaches out and pulls us up, just as He did with Peter.

Truth in Action

Where do you find yourself today? Do you feel like Peter, struggling to trust Christ's presence, protection, and saving power? Perhaps you are being consumed with fear as you see the storm swirling about you. Maybe your doubting is your faith being tested in a way you never thought possible. Whatever place you find yourself in, know that Christ is with you. Whether you are getting up in the morning to face the day ahead, having to make a decision you don't want to make, or fighting through the circumstance when you lack the energy and strength, one thing is absolutely certain: Christ is there beside you.

You will know this to be true as you keep your eyes focused on Christ and your heart surrendered to Him. In doing this, you will be able to then define in your mind what you believe in your heart to be true. You will know that Christ is with you and is giving you the strength to face one more day. We see the promise of this in Isaiah 39:29-31.

Finally, remember to refuse to allow the fear to captivate and control you. If you give into fear, it can dictate your ability to trust God, and you may begin to believe the lie that says, "You are alone to face the fight." Instead, take the fear to God and let the cry of your heart be "Lord, save me!" As you do, choose to believe that just as He saved Peter, so He will save you.

Reflection/Journal

_____
_____
_____
_____
_____
_____
_____
_____
_____
_____
_____
_____
_____
_____
_____
_____
_____
_____
_____
_____
_____
_____
_____
_____
_____
_____
_____
_____
_____
_____

~ 9 ~

The Value of Life
Marianne

Therefore, if anyone is in Christ, he is a new creation; the old has
gone, the new has come!
—2 Corinthians 5:17

We've probably all seen the poster of the kitten barely hanging onto
a branch, dangling in midair. The caption reads something like,
"Lord, help me. I'm so tiny in a world so big." Do you ever feel that
way? Unwelcome problems you're facing can become magnified to
the point that they appear bigger—even too big for God to handle.
The beliefs you've held to may not be comforting. They may even
be challenged in ways you never thought possible. This certainly
was the case with me as I faced the life-altering circumstances of
my daughter's illness. Twelve years ago, a doctor told us he would
do his very best to help our daughter, but he didn't know if it would
be good enough. He forewarned us that the road ahead would most
likely get worse before it got better and said our faith could quite
possibly be shaken to its core. He was right.

The vacillating process of reaching for healing, grasping it,
and then watching it slip through our fingers was maddening. The
constant cry of my heart was, "Lord, what are You doing? Please
help me see what You want me to learn here." By my timetable,
the answers were slow in coming. All I could see to do for the time
being was to get up each day whether or not I felt like it. I knew my
daughter needed me. She needed to know she could count on me.

I started to realize, while it felt like life as we knew it would never reappear, maybe I was looking in the wrong direction. Maybe I was looking at the past with the proverbial rose-colored glasses. Hadn't I previously learned from my walk with the Lord not to dwell on the past? Was that only in relationship to sin, or was it possible I needed to look at applying that in my present circumstances? I remembered God saying in Isaiah 55:8 that His thoughts were not my thoughts, neither my ways His. That much was apparent. It soon became clear to me that I needed to have an attitude adjustment: an attitude of the heart.

I was willing to search the Scripture to see what God had to say about lives that were in crisis. I wanted to know His thoughts and receive His guidance in regard to the challenges. Time was a precious commodity for me. Finding time to sit and pray would be a monumental feat. I asked God to help me see how I needed to rearrange my day to whatever degree I could. Someone suggested I didn't need to spend long time periods with God. Just a few minutes here and there throughout my day would make a difference. I began to "talk" to God in little snippets. But I didn't want to bother Him with the mundane details of my daily life. As I reached out to Him, oftentimes in desperation, I saw small positive changes. Mostly it had to do with my own viewpoint of how things were going. Watching details being attended to, especially seemingly small ones, encouraged me. Slowly, I decided to trust God with more things, some of the bigger ones. After all, if He could and would handle the little things, maybe He wanted to affect the big things as well. My heart attitude changed for the better, and my viewpoint followed. As I stepped out in faith, talking to God, telling Him about my day and my concerns, I felt my trust level growing. I was beginning to realize it wasn't so much about having the past back as it was creating a new future and a new normal for my family and myself.

It was becoming clear to me that the value of life wasn't to be measured by the circumstances I encountered. Life's value wouldn't be found in living life as it had always been but rather in accepting what was and eventually looking forward to what lay ahead. The value of life isn't found in the things we do or what we've experienced but simply in the fact that God gave us life. Life is incredibly valuable by virtue of its existence, whether in the here and now or in the eternal sense. I was learning I had a choice as to how I would handle the circumstances and what I would do with what I was given. Peace would be found inside of me rather than around me. As I came to understand this more, I found I was able to "hang on" a little better. I felt less like the kitty on the poster. I even began to enjoy quiet time in the many moments accumulated throughout the day. I found, just as Jesus did, that as I kept in constant contact with my Father God, His presence was what shaped me. It gave me courage. It didn't happen overnight. Eventually I found I was living in the new normal, with all it had to offer. Some of my preconceptions about life and God were challenged, but that was part of the very process I needed to walk though. Life was never to be the same, but it transitioned to a new life, one with joys and tears, just like the old one. I realized just as some things change, other things remain the same, no matter where I found myself in the journey. What was different was the character Christ was shaping within me, a character that was hopefully more of a reflection of Him. Just as promised, in 2 Corinthians 5:17, "Therefore, if anyone is in Christ, he is a new creation; the old has gone, the new has come!"

Truth in Action

If we are going to keep on going in the daily battles we face and find value in the life we are living, our hearts and minds have to be purposeful. If we choose to focus on the difficulties of life, we will certainly miss the simple beauty and truths right in front of us. One of those truths is God's desire to shape our character in the midst of the circumstances of life. If we are to take Him at His word, we must let Him do what He needs to do despite how things appear to be going. In the first chapter of the book of James, we are told to remember that the testing of our faith develops perseverance, and perseverance must finish its work so that we can be "mature and complete." If that seems foreign to you, ask God to show you how this work can play out in your life in the place where you presently find yourself. As you see God's hand in your life, you will get to know Him in ways not previously understood. Part of getting to know God is experiencing Him in the many circumstances or paths of our lives. Clearly, you may not always understand God or what He is doing. Ask Him to help you see what you may be missing. Ask Him to give you encouragement and make Himself known. He will; He's just waiting for you to ask.

If you are facing an uncertain future, with the possibility that life as you once knew it will never return, be certain that you do not have to do it alone. You have a Father who loves and understands you. He knows the tears you've cried, the anger you've held onto, and the disappointments you need to let go of. When you are ready, He will help you in the process. God's Word tells us He is compassionate and He will never leave us to face the challenges alone. If you look at verses 15-16 of Isaiah 49, you see God comforting His people just as a mother does her child, but there is a surprising difference stated. We read, in verse 15, "Can a mother forget the baby at her breast and have no compassion on the child she has borne? Though she may forget you, I will not forget you! See, I have engraved you on the palms of my hands . . ." Can there be any greater love or compassion shown than that shown by Jesus, who died a death He didn't deserve so we could have a life we could never earn? Although our lives may not always look the way we imagine they should, and we will inevitably face circumstances that appear insurmountable, we have the promises written for us that we will forever have the presence and compassion of a faithful God. Trust Him to work in your life and in your heart in His own time to help you see where the true value of life is found.

Reflection/Journal

~ 10 ~

Either Take Her or Heal Her
Marianne

> "'For I know the plans I have for you,' declares the Lord, 'plans to prosper you and not to harm you, plans to give you hope and a future.'"
> —Jeremiah 29:11

"Either take her or heal her!" I yelled out in utter frustration. My heart had been broken for what seemed like an eternity now. I was tired of facing the unknowns. The state of my daughter's health was not good. It seemed no matter what progress we made, there was inevitably a setback headed our way. My emotions were raw, and waiting patiently was no longer a mantra I wanted to live by. The days that turned into weeks, then months, were now being realized in terms of years. I had had enough.

My emotions, fears, doubts, and anger were rushing to the surface. I wasn't even sure I cared what the impact would be in terms of my relationship with God. Where I was concerned, life needed to make a drastic turn for the better, and immediately wasn't soon enough. As I yelled out to God, I couldn't stop the tears I had held back. Rushing like torrential waters, the tears spilled down my face. I wasn't aware of the presence of the one to whom my fury was directed. But He was there in that moment, just as He had been every day. Waiting patiently me for me to notice Him, He let the waves of sadness overtake me. He knew I needed to let go, and He was willing to let me *vent*, as it is so commonly known today.

41

By the time I stopped crying, I knew there was nothing else to do but give up and give in. I wouldn't be able to change the course of things with my anger. Nonetheless, I needed desperately to let go of it, and to be honest with the one I was blaming, subconsciously. When people asked, "How are you holding up?" I gave the standard answer, "Oh okay, I guess. God is faithful . . ." But as of recently, I wasn't clinging to that truth. My reality had become a living nightmare, and I just wanted the nightmare to end. I was feeling emotionally battered and was tired of trudging on, not so bravely anymore.

As I sat in a crumpled heap on the floor, I exclaimed with deep anguish, "God, I give up. I can't seem to control things anymore. I'm tired of seeing my daughter be bounced back and forth like a yo-yo with health concerns." There were too many to enumerate, and I knew God didn't need me to list them all off. He waited for me to say what was truly on my mind. Slowly, with agonizing honesty, I asked, "God, where are You? Have You abandoned me?" And as I did, a silence fell over the room, not yet a peace. I was no longer willing to try to keep my daughter with me. I realized, as God gently spoke to my spirit, that she wasn't mine to keep. With a broken but surrendered heart, I gave her over to the one who had given her life. I knew it would be better, at that point, for her to live in eternity with the Savior she had given her life to than for me to demand that she stay here with her family at any cost. The truth of the state of my heart was devastating. I was no longer trusting the one who lent me my child. I was trying to fix it all, and God had no choice but to back off for a while. He did not leave; He just let me do what I was choosing to do. After all, it was my choice to make, not His. He knew He couldn't control, nor would He control, my heart if I was not willing to let Him. God knows it's not about control but about love. I had yet to learn that lesson.

It was in those moments of surrender that I came to know the love of Jesus as my friend. I had trusted Jesus to save me from an eternity without Him. But had I trusted Him to live His life through me? I had read, many times before, the words of Jeremiah, the namesake of my oldest child. When God spoke to him in Jeremiah

29:11-13, He told him He had plans for life. The words were now echoing in my heart, and not only in my brain. Instead of Jeremiah's name, I heard my own, "Marianne, I know the plans I have for you, plans to prosper you and not to harm you, plans to give you hope and a future. Then you will call upon Me, and come and pray to Me, and I will listen to you." Wait, did I hear that correctly or remember it accurately from the Bible? It continued, "You will seek Me and find Me when you seek Me with all your heart."

Wow, the reality hit like a baseball coming out of midair to strike at my heart. Thud! There it was, the truth. God hadn't abandoned me. He wasn't surprised at what was happening. He hadn't thrown up His arms in the air, exclaiming that all was lost. *No,* He was reminding me He had a plan for my life and for my daughter's life. Furthermore, the plan wasn't for harm, discouragement, or destruction but for hope and a future! Oh, how I needed to hear that, to be reminded of God's unending love and faithfulness. But there was more I needed to hear. Jeremiah clearly tells us that we will seek God and find Him when we seek Him with all our heart. It was evident that I had not been seeking God with all my heart. I was too caught up in the cares and concerns of life that Jesus told me not to worry about (1 Peter 5:7). I remembered now, "each day has enough troubles of its own," Jesus had said in His Word (Matthew 6:34). Why was I inviting more by worrying?

As I sat on the floor, I confessed my worry, doubts, and lack of trust to God. My heart was a little lighter. I realized the future wasn't mine to control. But God, lovingly and with tender compassion, let me get to the bottom of my worries, and then He reminded me how very much He loved me. I knew as I read over the words of Jeremiah 29 that my fears were unfounded. Did I need to give my daughter to Him? Most certainly, she wasn't "mine" in the first place. But I had claimed her for my own. Now I gave her back, trusting that the same God who loved me, had a plan for me, and would never abandon me would undoubtedly do the same for her. I was learning to claim, along with Horatio Spafford, the words, "It is well, it is well with my soul."

Truth in Action

Is your heart burdened to the point of desperation? Are you feeling like maybe you've been abandoned? Take heart! God has not nor will He ever abandon you. Will He deliver you from all your troubles soon? Probably not. But He will *not leave you alone* in them. If we look at the last physical encounter of Jesus and His disciples, as described in Matthew 28, we see confused, perhaps dismayed, and even somewhat hopeless followers. Their world had recently been turned upside down, and now it appeared Jesus was once again leaving and they were not sure what to do. Jesus did not chastise or belittle them. Rather, He inspired hope in their hearts. He gave them truth and instructions of what their next steps should be.

First, He let them know all authority "in heaven and on earth" had been given to Him. In other words, He addressed their concerns by helping them have a different perspective of the recent life changes. He wanted them to see the very unexpected happenings were not a sign of things being out of the control of a loving father, but rather the circumstances surrounding His death allowed Jesus to take control for the world that so needed Him. Second, He let them know what their next steps needed to be as they faced life without His physical presence. They had a mission, a life-altering, eternity giving journey they needed to be attending to. He gave them what some call "the great commission." Jesus told His followers to spread the news of His resurrection and life to all the world.

In a time when life was looking bleak, Jesus was able to redirect the hearts of the friends He loved so very much while letting them know He would be with them forever, and He would never leave them. His final words were for their comfort, to reassure them of the truth that He would never abandon them: "And surely I am with you always, to the very end of the age." Did you catch that? He didn't say, "Go out and do what I tell you, and then I will be with you." He knew the state of their hearts, their questions, and the processes they would each be going through. He reassured them that as they took the steps forward they needed to, He *is* with them. Those words are for you today. He's waiting for you to come to Him. If you're dismayed, perhaps angry, or brokenhearted, He is here for you. He won't be shocked. He will, however, want you to get to the bottom of what is truly going on, just as He did with me. It's only there when you surrender everything, including what you are most hanging onto, that He can calm the storm within you. The surrender may be bitter, but the healing will be sweet. Jesus loves you, my friend, and He's waiting for you.

Read through Jeremiah 29:11-13, Matthew 28:20, and Romans 8:28. God doesn't promise this life will be free of trials, temptations, and suffering, but He does assure us He can and will bring good out of everything His children encounter. He promises to be with you through all of it, as He says He is with us always, even to the end of time. Ask God to show you His plans for you, to make clear to you the good He wants to bring to your life. He wants you to know His presence, to give you peace that will sustain you. He longs to deliver you from the worries that surround you. Just as I had to learn, you too need to know the power of believing, claiming the words written on the pages of the Bible as truth for your life.

Reflection/Journal

~ 11 ~

He Is Tangible
Mary Rose

He tends His flock like a shepherd: He gathers the lambs in His arms and carries them close to His heart; He gently leads those that have young.
—Isaiah 40:11-12

Are you in a place in life where you are hurting, feeling alone, or perhaps struggling through what have become the routines of life and are desperately searching to feel and see God in a tangible way? You may know and hold faith that God is hearing your prayers, but are feeling frustrated and lost at what appears to be a lack of response from God. If you are in such a place, then read on; there is hope yet.

I have been in places that felt like trudging through desert, only to find myself in a quicksand of emotions. The years of battling my illness were nearly the worst. Looking back, I remember how routine things became; I ate three meals around the same time frames every day, Mom and I did devotions almost every morning, I watched movie after movie, I took medications at set times, and I fell asleep late, only to start it all over the next day. I was frustrated, I was tired, and I was done with living life in such physical pain, emotional confusion, and spiritual trial. I needed to see God in a tangible form. I needed to know He could be visible to me.

As I prayed, asking God to show Himself to me as someone I could literally see, He did. He did this in an extravagant way and in smaller ways, but all were confirming of His physical presence. I awoke early one morning, sometime around 2:00 or 3:00 a.m., and as I opened my eyes, I saw a light in the corner of my bedroom. It was not a light coming from any lamp. It was the light of illumination flowing from a physical being. There, Christ stood in the corner of my room with arms stretched wide. More amazingly, He didn't just stand there, He spoke, not in an audible voice, but one I heard and understood inwardly. He told me I didn't need to be afraid because He was with me. I didn't know what to say; no words could escape my mouth. I just laid there in awe. I closed my eyes for a moment, and when I reopened them, He was gone—visibly, I mean. I knew He was there; I just could not any longer see Him.

That moment during my illness was one of the most amazing ways God showed me His physical presence, and yet He continued to show me His tangibility in other ways. I saw His servant's heart when my parents fed me, I saw Him providing when people brought us meals, I saw His compassion when my friend would sit in silence next to me, and I saw His love through the thousands who prayed for me.

Since that time, I have faced similar and not-so-similar circumstances where the physical presence of God, my Daddy, is what I hungered for and needed in the depths of my soul. I found myself in the midst of a life storm a few years back. I was feeling as though I was utterly alone. It was a time of much confusion and pain. I remember feeling sheer desperation for someone to hold and embrace me as I cried one night, yet I believed I had no one to do so. This night in particular is one I will never forget. As I lay in my bed sobbing and feeling completely alone, I asked God to hold me in His arms as I fell asleep. I pleaded with Him, saying, "Daddy, please, please let me feel Your embrace," and in those moments and hours, I felt the physical arms of Christ wrapped around my body. I looked behind and in front of me, and He was not visible, but He was tangible. That night my heavenly Father gave me a gift, that of falling asleep in His arms. It is a gift that will never leave my memory.

Those nights, experiencing the visual sight and physical embrace of Christ, remind me that as I continue to face difficulties and trials, God is real and He has not left me. Since that time, He has continually shown me, through the small things in life and by meeting my everyday needs, that He is a God I can and do come in physical contact with continually.

Truth in Action

To know God tangibly is a thirst we all have innately within us. It's a hunger at the core of who we are and a desire we seek to have met, especially when facing difficulties. The interesting part to me is how we, as humans, continually face trials in life. They may come in the form of physical pain, emotional confusion, spiritual doubt and waywardness, or even death itself. No matter the circumstance, though, we are usually fighting through something. God doesn't want us to suffer and be in pain, but He does want us to learn more about Him. He wants us to trust that He will, "provide for those who grieve in Zion-to bestow on them a crown of beauty instead of ashes, the oil of gladness instead of mourning, and a garment of praise instead of a spirit of despair," as He promises in Isaiah 61:3.

God lets us know in His Word that He has chosen us for a specific purpose. He wants us to fight through the trials of life we are facing to better understand His purpose. Amazingly enough, God trusts you and me to endure and allow Him to conquer the battle through Christ. We will not win battles on our own, but we will win because Christ is empowering us and fighting through us. As we stand and fight, praying God's words aloud and choosing to believe their truth, we crush the enemy. When that happens, the lies that have held us captive lose their power over us, and God is victorious!

If you are struggling through life and the trials have weighed you down to the point where to see God in His physical being is nearly impossible, it's time you take up the sword of the spirit, spoken of in Ephesians 6! It is the Word of God. In His Word is truth that our enemy cannot escape. The desire to know God closely, as someone tangible, is not out of reach for you or any of us. In fact, it's a desire He put in our souls, a hunger to know Him in such a profound way that nothing else could match it or even come close.

As you pray and ask God to become visible to you, have faith and know He will. It may come in literally seeing or feeling Him, or it may be in other ways, but know He is showing Himself to you. Think of when you cry and need someone to hold you and someone does; that is Christ holding you. When you have had a bad day or you need someone to talk to and suddenly a friend calls or stops by; that is Christ reaching out to you. Or think about when you are stressed to the max and out of the blue someone says something that makes you burst into laughter; that is Christ making you laugh.

Now look at creation. Walk outside—go ahead. Let the wind dance around you; that's Christ softly grazing your arm. Listen to the trees rustle; that's Christ singing to you. Look at the vast sky above you; that's Christ saying, "I love you further than this spans," and when the sun sets this evening or rises in the morning, know that God says, "I painted this for you." Psalm 19:1-2 says, "The heavens declare the glory of God; the skies proclaim the work of his hands. Day after day they pour forth speech; night after night they display knowledge." Bask in His love and know He is with you at every turn, going up every steep climb and walking beside ready to carry you through. He is tangible.

Reflection/Journal

_____
_____
_____
_____
_____
_____
_____
_____
_____
_____
_____
_____
_____
_____
_____
_____
_____
_____
_____
_____
_____
_____
_____
_____
_____
_____
_____
_____
_____

~ 12 ~

Celebrate Life
Marianne

Give thanks in all circumstances, for this is God's will for you in
Christ Jesus.
—1 Thessalonians 5:18

In the darkest moments of our trials, it can be all too easy to forget
to celebrate. That was the place I found myself in twelve years ago.
As time spent fighting an illness was marching on, I was struggling
to find joy in anything in life. Survival was what I decided to
concentrate on.

Late one evening, I was asking God to please send some
encouragement my way. As I sat praying, I remembered the story of
a woman who, at a young age, was in a diving accident. She was left a
quadriplegic as a result of the accident. Her name was Joni Eareckson
Tada. I remembered seeing her speak on television at a Billy Graham
Crusade. She had a joy I couldn't understand at that moment. I
wondered how someone in a wheelchair, as my daughter now was,
could say she would rather spend her life in a wheelchair and know
Jesus than to be able to walk and be without Him. I decided, at that
moment, I wanted to try and contact her.

My search began via the Internet. As I typed in her name, a
site popped up called Joni and Friends. I left a message for her,
explaining our family's circumstances, and asked if she had any

52

thoughts or encouragement to offer. The words she wrote back to me reverberate in my mind with their truth even to this day.

Joni's simple yet wisdom-filled advice came from God's Word but spoke of her own life's experience. Joni encouraged me to learn to be thankful in the midst of my circumstances. She pointed out how in the Bible, Paul called the people of the Thessalonian church to be thankful in every circumstance. Paul made a life-changing suggestion that would apply to all people, in all circumstances. Joni explained we are not called to be happy *for* the circumstance but *in* it. She said it wasn't that she was particularly thankful to be in a wheelchair, but she was eternally grateful for having come to know Jesus. She talked of how she knew the truth that Jesus would never leave her. In Matthew 28:20, Jesus tells His disciples He will never leave them, even to the end of the age. Joni had come to learn the truth of His Word in her own life. Her unwavering belief in Jesus served to deepen my faith that if He could take care of her, He would take care of us.

Joni also challenged me to start looking for the many ways God was reaching out, to show His deep love and compassion. As I accepted her challenge and asked God to show Himself to me, I began to celebrate life again. My eyes were opened up to the realization that friends around me were sent to be the hands and feet of Jesus. I pondered the incredible faithfulness of a friend who weekly came to get my laundry and later would drop it back off clean and folded. She quietly left the basket of fresh-smelling clothes on our front porch, so as not to disturb the family. This remarkable gift of service went on for an entire year. Yes, God was showing Himself to be faithful. I only had to open my eyes to the gift right before me.

Although our family's circumstances did not change quickly for the better, or even in seemingly significant ways, all at once, it was again the attitude of my heart that led me to see life differently. Instead of mourning over the loss of things in the midst of the trials, I started to see the simple blessings of everyday life, blessings I knew God was giving as His gifts of love. As I found myself worn out, inevitably the phone would ring and someone would offer to come sit with my daughter so I could get a little time to myself. As if by magic, someone would stop by with a meal for our family. I often had no idea what to say to friends who came with food, money, or an offer to clean my house. Some wanted to just spend time with our daughter so we could take our son out for a little fun. These kindnesses often came with no prompting on my part or my family's part. But they came usually when we were in need of whatever it was they were offering. Many would say they weren't sure why they were doing what they were, attributing it only to a feeling or sense that it was what we needed at the moment. It was all evidence to me of hearts moved by the compassion and love of the God who promised to care for His children.

I was learning a very valuable lesson. As I opened the eyes of my heart to seeing the blessings being offered, I gained strength in the joy I let myself feel. The understanding of how important it was to celebrate the seemingly little things of life was becoming clearer. In the celebration of the moment, my heart was lifted and the burden lightened. A lighter, freer heart caused me to look less for the next awful thing to happen and instead to anticipate the next victory to be found. I was, as a result, better equipped to handle the challenges as they came. Learning to be thankful in my circumstance still comes with difficulty at times. But as I remember the advice given by Joni, I continue to look for how God is answering my requests for help. Most often, it comes in ways I would not think to ask for, but the answers seem to be better than I could hope to receive.

Truth in Action

If you are in the midst of life-challenging circumstances, know that you are not alone. God has promised to be our hope. In Psalm 46:1, we read, "God is our refuge and strength, an ever-present help in trouble." Help may not always come in the forms you ask for, but it will be there for you. I wasn't sure of exactly what I needed for encouragement, but God knew what I required and He always sent hope in the form He knew best. You can trust Him to do that for you. You don't have to figure it all out on your own. When your encouragement comes, in whatever form it may be, remember to celebrate! Even the seemingly small things will give hope for your tomorrows.

If rest is what you need, God promises, in verses 1-2 of Psalm 62, to be that rest and a rock that we can count on: "My soul finds rest in God alone; my salvation comes from him. He alone is my rock and my salvation; he is my fortress, I will never be shaken." You can take God at His word, even if you need to ask Him to help you see how He is working on your behalf. If you need encouragement, try to look for specific things each day that God is doing in your life. As you open your eyes to see Him caring for you, thank Him. Just as Joni taught me, learn to be thankful in your circumstance, even if it's not possible for you to feel thankful for it. As you purpose to see and recognize God's hand in your life, reaching out to lift the burdens, your load will be lightened, just as mine often was. You will find yourself better prepared as you continue to face each day with all it may hold. God wants to be your safe place, your strength to face each day and new challenge, and the help that reaches out to carry you through.

Reflection/Journal

_____

_____

_____

_____

_____

_____

_____

_____

_____

_____

_____

_____

_____

_____

_____

_____

_____

_____

_____

_____

_____

_____

_____

_____

_____

_____

_____

~ 13 ~

New Blessings to Strengthen the Spirit
Mary Rose

A man of many companions may come to ruin, but there is a
friend who sticks closer than a brother.
—Proverbs 18:24

There are those times in life when we feel as though we have hit
a brick wall. It's as if we are spinning our wheels, yet not moving
forward, similar to a hamster on a wheel. For some of us, we may
be struggling with our sin or addiction. Perhaps for others it is
working through to heal a relationship or coping with the loss
of a loved one. Still, for many of us it may be that our walk with
Christ has become mundane and regimented, losing its fervor
and excitement. Yet, no matter the struggle, it can leave us feeling
frustrated and stuck if we have been trying to overcome, heal, or
nurture it for some time.

It's in these times where God shows up in the best yet somewhat
unexpected way. He comes to us through a friend, but even more so,
He comes in the form of a friend in need of our help. After reading
this, you might be perplexed, confused even, but stop and think
about it for a moment. He brings someone into our lives who needs
our help, encouragement, and strength in order to in turn give us
the very things we need. It is an incredible gift, not one to be bought
or one the world can offer. It is simply the gift of being there for
another. It's beginning to make sense, isn't it?

Over the years, I have faced various situations, and it has been through helping, loving, and supporting others that I myself have found encouragement and strength to face my circumstance. Most of the time, God tends to bring into my life those who are new to their walk with Him or those who are struggling with their walk. Those who are new to the faith provide me with such an encouragement when my relationship with Jesus is in a time of drought. God uses them to take me back to the basics of what I know to be true of His character but have slowly forgotten. Most of us can remember what a fervor we had for Christ when we first came to Him, and perhaps you're in that now. What I love and find so endearing about that time is it's the beginning of our love affair with Christ. For those of us facing times of doubt, confusion, and brokenness, God uses another person's faith and fervor to reignite passion in us. As this happens, God heals our hearts and restores our faith's firm foundation.

For those who are struggling in their walk with God, we are asked to come alongside them, to lift them up. As we do this, pointing the way back to God with the grace and compassion only He can give, we, in turn, are lifted up. It happens as we are reminded of God's incredible love for us. His love resonates in the other person, which in turn provides us with renewed strength and hope that we too can overcome our struggle.

Have you ever experienced the joy of helping someone else? It's a joy you can't explain, but you gain it when you are able to provide something for someone in need. It doesn't matter, either, if it's a helping hand, a shoulder to cry on, or a listening ear you give. The joy goes further into us, though, and creates a peace within our souls, does it not? When we are given the gift of helping someone else for God, it penetrates our hearts to help heal us. Slowly, little by little, God uses their circumstances or as is the case with some, the beginnings of their faith to remind us of God's faithfulness and healing power in our own lives.

Truth in Action

Do you find yourself struggling to make it through life? Are you doubting your choices in life, focusing on the mistakes you have made, or dwelling in the sorrow of loss? Know that Christ has not left you. Pray and ask Him to remind you of this truth, that you are His and no matter what, He is always and forever with you. As you do this, you will see the tangibility of God reaching out through another. Sometimes God will bring people into our lives only for a time. We are meant to help them and they are meant to help us for that time in our lives. Yet sometimes God will allow a beautiful friendship to grow from this bond of helping one another. The awesome thing about this is being given the gift of seeing God paint each life into a beautiful painting. It's a picture of His love, grace, and friendship.

Finally, remember the truth that God gives us friends, but even greater He calls us His friends in John 15:15: "I no longer call you servants, because a servant does not know his master's business. Instead, I have called you friends, for everything that I learned from my Father I have made known to you." Therefore, we have the amazing gift of Christ as our constant friend. His friendship is abiding, meaning constant. We have access to all of Christ every minute of the day. If it's a father you need, He is that. If it is a brother, He is that as well. If it's a friend you need, He will show Himself in the form of a friendship with another. Ultimately, no matter what we need, He is all-sufficient and He is will supply our every need.

Reflection/Journal

~ 14 ~

An Awakening of the Heart
Marianne

I have told you these things, so that in me you may have peace. In
this world you will have trouble. But take heart! I have overcome
the world.

—John 16:33

Our first Christmas after Mary Rose's diagnosis was met with many
emotions, not the least of which was sadness. I wanted to have a
normal routine for the holidays. We were not able to go places as a
family because my daughter could only have very limited contact
with people due to concerns about her immune system. Watching
the sadness grow in Mary Rose's eyes led me to thinking about what
we could do to divert her attention. What better way to do that than
to put on a favorite Christmas movie? My choice was the classic *It's a
Wonderful Life* with Jimmy Stewart. As we sat watching the movie, I
began to reflect on the messages being played out before me.

We watched Jimmy Stewart as the main character, George
Bailey, struggle through his disappointment with how things had
turned out in life and come to a new heart attitude by the end of this
epic film. I imagine many who have seen this movie have had some
of the same emotions as I encountered. I felt sadness over George's
dilemma, shock and indignation toward the miserly banker who
wouldn't return the lost money, curiosity over how George would
come to see what the viewer could plainly observe, and finally, joy

61

at the outcome of George's circumstances. How exciting to follow the transformation!

Watching this simple story was like viewing my own life's story in many ways. It wasn't that the particular circumstances were the same. The basic human dilemma about how life often doesn't seem to be going the way we had planned was more of what I could relate to. I was in a time of trying my very best to work things out. My best didn't seem to be good enough, though. It didn't stop my daughter from getting sick, and it wasn't necessarily helping her get any better. Unlike George in the movie, I wasn't struggling with the idea of ending my life but with becoming resigned to the circumstances surrounding me. The death I was seeking wasn't to my body physically; it was to my feelings, to my soul. I was tired of being sad, frustrated, fearful, even jealous, feeling as if everyone around me was living life but mine was passing me by. There was no doubt I, like George Bailey, needed to see life from a different perspective. I just wasn't sure how to make it happen.

In a Christmas correspondence, a friend asked me if I could still see God as being faithful and good despite what was happening to our family. I wrote back telling her I didn't see God as being the one to blame for what was happening. But in reality, wasn't that exactly what I was doing as my attitude and heart sank lower into numbness? That is a particular danger for those facing long-term circumstances or life changes. I needed to find a way to get my heart back on track. I pondered what had happened in *It's a Wonderful Life*. George's life had certainly taken some very unexpected turns, and he needed to be reminded that goodness in people still existed and his own life was of more value than he thought it to be. Short of asking for a do-over in life, I needed to somehow see life as being valuable right where God had me. I sensed He had me right where He wanted me. But I wasn't sure where I was to be heading. I began to think about the meaning behind Christmas, asking God to remind me of the importance of Christ's coming.

As my mind wandered back to the present, I began to pay more attention to the movie we were watching. I paid special attention to those who were sent to help rescue George. The angel, Clarence, was not exactly who one would think could do the job he was sent to do, which was to help George see his value as a person. Hmm, that was a little familiar. Hadn't the people of Jesus's time thought it absurd that anyone coming from Nazareth could have anything of value to say, let alone to do? After all, Jesus was not exactly the king everyone thought they should be looking for. In the movie, it was through Clarence's compassion, obedience to God, and focused goal that George would find out the true meaning of his own life. He was valuable just for who he was, and his mere existence gave his life its value. His job, house, and life savings didn't determine his worth. Things might not have looked as George thought they should, but it wasn't about his expectations. It was about a man seeing the blessings around him and realizing he wouldn't be left alone to deal with life's worst. It also was about the human heart, which was portrayed through the town's people, being moved by compassion to jump in where needed to help out a fellow man. As I thought about how my life had unfolded and the disappointment I was feeling, I realized it really wasn't about me. It was about Him, Jesus. He was the one who brought people to help our family. He was the one who answered my cry to find a doctor who could tell us what was really happening to our daughter. He was the one who showed up on the doorstep in the form of little children to sing Christmas carols to us to cheer us all. He was the one who held the answers to my own personal dilemmas, as well the answers being sought by a hurting world.

As I realized I had been missing the whole message of Christmas, I was moved to look anew to what God had done in the Bible. I needed to get a better understanding of the love Christ offered me. As I searched God's Word, I looked at Isaiah 9. I read over the descriptions of God: Wonderful Counselor, Prince of Peace. I asked God to give me a new appreciation of who He was for me. That was when my heart became softened to the truth of an incredible Savior who, for the love of humankind, for love of me, agreed to leave His throne in heaven. Jesus trusted His father with the outcome of His very life here on earth. If Jesus, who was God, could humble Himself to accept His Father's plans and willingly submit to them, who was I to question the plans God had laid out for me? As I searched further, I came upon Psalm 139. It all came together there for me.

My heart was broken and in awe to read that God knew me before I was in the womb. I was thought to be a treasure by God before I even came to be. Wow! The understanding of that was foreign to me. God already knew what I would live through and how it would all unfold. He knew when and how my heart would be broken and become rebellious toward Him. He was willing to come and meet me right where I was. I was loved before my time began, and nothing I could do would ever change that.

As the movie came to an end that evening, my ponderings led me to realize George Bailey wasn't the only one who needed to accept the fact that he was a treasure to others. I needed to be reminded of God's love for me and my family and that He was reaching out to us and would continue to handle things as we let Him take the reins. I don't remember thinking, *Yep, it's a wonderful life,* but I do recall having a renewed sense of joy and peace that Christmas. My heart was in awe of a love so encompassing. I was learning that my life and the future of our family could be entrusted to Jesus, our Wonderful Counselor, Mighty God, Everlasting Father, and Prince of Peace.

Truth In Action

Perhaps you are in a place of painful awareness that your life is not turning out the way you envisioned. Despite your very best efforts, you cannot seem to change the circumstances around you, like George Bailey. If that is where you find yourself, much like the place I found myself, it's time for you to let God renew your spirit and give you a new understanding of how very much He loves you. You are a treasure to God and to those around you. You may be standing at a crossroads in your life. You can choose to let the pain and circumstances make you bitter or even spiteful. There is another choice, however, another path you can choose. It will be tough at first because it will be foreign to you, just as it was to me. Don't give up! It will get better. It will not always be as hard as it is right now.

In God's word, we see Jesus constantly reassuring His disciples He is with them, and they will not face the suffering alone. In John 16:33, Jesus tells His followers and us, "I have told you these things, so that in me you may have peace. In this world you will have trouble. But take heart! I have overcome the world." As you venture on this path with God, you will find rest for your mind, peace in your soul, and renewed hope for your future. Be honest with God. Tell Him you're struggling, but don't stop there. Dive into His Word, as I had to do. Take some time to read again, or for the very first time, what God wants you to know in Psalm 139. Just as He did with me, God wants you to see how He knew you, loved you, and planned for you and will never let you go, no matter how far away you may try to run. Like the character George Bailey, maybe it is time for you to learn *who* you really are and the value your life holds. Let God speak to your heart and show you how He sees you and the intrinsic value of your life.

Reflection/Journal

~ 15 ~

The Great Romance
Mary Rose

The Lord your God is with you, His is mighty to save. He will
take great delight in you, He will quiet you with His love, He will
rejoice over you with singing.
—Zephaniah 3:17

We as people long to be loved. We as woman strive to be captivating
and interesting and ultimately, to be cherished. When a woman
leaves the man who loves her breathless, she feels treasured, one of
a kind, and unlike any other. Men strive to be valiant, strong, and
greatly respected. When a man becomes a hero for the woman he
loves, he feels accomplished and appreciated. He becomes the one
she runs to for protection, safety, and love.

Far greater than these rooted desires, though, lies the longing in
the depths of our soul for a love affair with Jesus. If you are a man
reading this, the last sentence may have taken you by surprise; that's
okay. The love affair you most long for is to know that your heavenly
Father can and does love you. For us as women, the love affair we
yearn for is to be deeply loved by Jesus. It's to know He will fight for
us and to know we captivate Him.

I have been a Christian for seventeen years now, since I was five
years old, and I have experienced many depths to my relationship
with Christ. Yet none compare to having a love affair with Him.
Christ is said to be our Bridegroom in the Bible, the one who actually
yearns for us, longs to know the deep oceans of our heart, and

searches for us in the thicket of the forest. He sacrifices everything He has to go in search for us. He did so when He died for us, and He continues to do so now.

Throughout my walk with Christ, there have been two times, and the third is now unfolding, where He has shown me the different ways He is my bridegroom. He first became my friend, then my beloved, and finally He will become my groom. Coming to know Him as my friend began during my illness. Much of my time was occupied by my lying in bed or just sitting in silence, which led me to feeling incredibly alone. It was not because people had abandoned me, because to tell the truth, it was the opposite in that way. I felt alone because my childhood was slipping away from me due to the disease I was fighting. I would look out my window and see kids playing next door. I could hear the sound of their laughter, and I knew that was the closest I would get to participating in those years of my childhood.

When my friends came to visit, it was usually bittersweet for me. They would share with me what they were doing in school, what sports they were playing, and, eventually, what boy they were interested in. As much as I wanted to know what the outside world was doing, it also pained me to hear it because I couldn't participate in anything.

It was at that time Jesus became my dearest friend. He was the one who did the daily tasks with me. He endured all the pain, fear, sadness, and confusion with me. He sat with me when I ate, He spoke to me when I read His Word, and He gave me hope that one day I would have normalcy in life again. As difficult and trying as my illness was, Christ used that time to reveal to me the first layer of His love for me, beginning in friendship.

A few years later, as our friendship grew and tragedy struck, He slowly became my beloved. At age fifteen, I unexpectedly lost two close friends in a car accident. I was left feeling distraught, angry, and confused over the whole reality of what had happened. During that time of heartbreak, I screamed, I questioned, and I badgered Christ for answers, some of which He showed me and others I may never know. Yet through that, Jesus grew close to me, and I grew close to Him. I began to realize no matter what I felt, what I said, or how I doubted, Christ was ever-present. I also learned, in a new way, how precious life was and how I dearly wanted to experience deep love in life.

Interests in boys came and went, with nothing coming of them, yet one remained constant: Christ. He sought after me, and He persuaded me. Jesus wanted me to know how lovely I am, how beautiful my face smiles, and how captivating my heart is. He wanted me to experience what being truly loved and pursued was before a man would come along to do so. Christ knew how important it was for me to have a solid relationship with Him first and to know He is my first love and will always be.

In June of 2010, I got engaged to the man I have been with since we were yet teenagers. I am preparing to enter into a love unlike any other in this life. A new journey of romance and divine love with Christ will begin. Slowly, Christ is revealing to me what that will mean. As a Christian woman, it was important that I came to know Christ first as a friend then as my beloved. Likewise, it has been essential that my fiancé be grounded in a friendship with Christ in order to be ready for marriage. No matter where you find yourself in your relationship with Christ, there is always a deeper level to be found, and it's yours for the taking.

Truth in Action

Are you in the place of life where you need a friend, and no matter who you turn to, you feel the connection is just not working? The encouragement you need, the shoulder you could use to cry on, or the listening ear, whatever the need, it's unable to be met. If this is you, have hope: Christ is that friend you are looking for! He has allowed others to be unable to help you because He wants to show you how He can be your friend. So I challenge you, ask Him to let you see how He cares for you. Pay attention to how He is trying to meet your need, and don't be afraid to talk to Him. Then be silent and wait for Him to reply.

Perhaps you're one who has a developed a deep friendship with Christ but you have not met Him as your beloved. Instead you have spent years waiting for Mr. Right and come shy every time, only to be left heartbroken and empty. If this is you, I have a promise of redemption for you. Christ has been pursuing you. The very thing you have longed for a man to do, Christ has been doing.

Christ is captivated by you. I know this may sound strange, but trust me, He is amazed by your beauty, and He wants you to be amazed by it too. Until you see this in yourself, you will not be ready to accept a man seeing it in you. So my challenge to you is this: let Christ shower you with His love. Allow Him to show you your value in Him. As Christ becomes your first love, then when you least expect it, He will bring the man who will love and be captivated by you.

Men, I do not have experience in your shoes, but what I do know of you is you long to be the beloved of a woman. You long to know her touch and the deep desires of her heart. Yet, you cannot understand this in a woman unless Christ has the depths of your heart first. So I challenge you men, don't look for a woman to fill your desires as a man; look to Christ. Allow Christ alone to show you your validation as a man.

Finally, for those of you who are married, widowed, divorced, or preparing for marriage, your groom is waiting for you. No matter which of these woman you are, Christ wants to have the first dance with you. He wants you to bask in His sacrificial love, and He wants you to know you are His bride, a treasure beyond compare. So for you women, now that Christ is your dearest friend and your beloved, let Him show you what it means to be your bridegroom. Allow Him to shower you with His love for you. When He becomes your bridegroom, it's not about your relationship with Him. Rather, it's about His relationship with you. He adores and loves you.

Reflection/Journal

~ 16 ~

Which Road Do We Choose, Lord?

Marianne

> He restores my soul. He guides me in paths of righteousness for
> His name's sake . . . You prepare a table before me in the presence
> of my enemies.
> —Psalm 23:3, 5

When you survey the map of your life, which encompasses every choice you've made or had to make, do you ever feel perhaps you've taken some wrong turns along the way? Have you made choices to take some paths you wished you hadn't? If you've lived for any length of time, chances are you will answer yes to the above questions. In fact, you may be faced with some life-changing decisions as you read the words written before you. A decision to move to the right or to the left on your personal roadmap of life could impact the days ahead in significant ways. Perhaps you already know that and have made a choice, fearful of the outcome. If any of this sounds familiar, read on, my friend.

Life makes many demands on us. People demand our attention, bosses give near-impossible deadlines, children max out our patience, and things in our homes break when the finances seem to be at their worst. Decisions have to be made on a daily basis. Some decisions are smaller, with fewer consequences; others are not. We may unexpectedly find ourselves at a fork in the road. We can choose to stay where we are, fearful of moving, or weigh out the options and hope for the best. But what happens when we have made decisions that don't appear to be working out the way we had hoped? Do we continue on the path or possibly try to forge another way?

My husband and I stood at one of those crossroads twelve years ago. We found ourselves having to consider a completely unfamiliar route. It could lead to a place of great uncertainty, with possible fatal consequences. The first of many decisions needed to be made in a fairly quick timeframe. Up until the actual correct diagnosis was given to our daughter's illness, we took our daughter from doctor to doctor and hospital to hospital, all with the same results: nothing. We were even told by a doctor who was, at the time, the head of a large family practice that perhaps some psychological testing needed to be done. When the therapist returned her diagnosis to the doctor stating our daughter was not ill because she was depressed but that she was heading toward depression because she was ill, the doctor was infuriated with her. The therapist made a call to our home, saying it was time for a new family doctor. A decision had to be made. Yet another doctor's advice needed to be sought. So far, we only seemed to be going in circles. We were desperately trying to find an answer but were not sure we really wanted to know the truth. We knew, however, we had no real choice but to continue on until we had the correct diagnosis.

The next doctor we saw diagnosed our daughter with advanced, acute Lyme disease. The suggested protocol would require a pick line be inserted into her left arm. It would run up her arm and end just above her heart. Medicine could then be dispensed at a frequent rate. It was medicine that was so powerful, it could potentially end our daughter's life from the effects alone. As scary as that sounds, the thought of staying where we were was not any more comforting. Mary Rose was rapidly losing weight as her body was being ravaged by an unseen killer within. Another choice had to be made within a few short days.

The trip to the hospital proved to be not only frustrating but also very painful for our daughter. A procedure that was only to take a couple of hours turned into a sixteen-hour fiasco. We could have easily second guessed ourselves. We knew that the doctor who suggested the protocol had had success with several patients, and we were determined to get on a better path. Watching our daughter in pain and seeing the plea in her eyes was almost more than we could bear. It was the very thing, however, that could lead to life. The path we were on previously was only leading to certain death.

Medicines were being dispensed. A home nurse came to check on our daughter and show us what to do. The doctor had forewarned us our daughter would get worse before she would get better. The reality of watching her tiny body be pumped with medicine and then seeing the effects it had on her were enough to make us question ourselves. After a night spent in the emergency room, watching as nurses and doctors tried frantically to dissolve a blood clot in her pick line, we were not at all convinced we had made the right choices. We were told if the clot did not dissolve and made its way to her heart, it would mean death. Had we, in fact, unwittingly sentenced our daughter to death? The agony of such questions drove my husband and myself to our knees. We pled with God to make it known whether we chose the right path. It was a very dark night of the soul, and many like it were to follow. We pled with God to comfort us with the knowledge we had made the right decisions.

After weeks of trying to decide what needed to be our next move, the answers to our hearts' cries came during a conversation with a friend. She was the same friend who had faced cancer with her son and had to make many similar choices. She listened to all I had to say and then slowly spoke with a knowing certainty. She asked if the path we were on previously had led to any real conclusions or positive results. The answer was a resounding *no!* She proceeded to remind me that we had done what we felt we needed to do to make a unified, concrete decision. My husband and I had sought advice from those who had dealt successfully with the illness and protocol. We had been on our knees in prayer, seeking God's wisdom. We had requested prayer from anyone around us who would pray. Finally, we were left to wait for an answer. The one forthcoming led us to the place we now found ourselves. We looked at the options and proceeded to move forward on what appeared to be the very best route. Given the circumstances of the time, we decided to trust the advice of those who had gone before us.

What we had not counted on was perhaps the reality we would face as a result of our new choices. We had to face the fact that what we were experiencing was not the result of bad choices or careless mistakes; it was what we had to face to get to a new and better place. We needed to stay on the path we had chosen and wait. The circumstances were not being governed by our *lack thereof*; they were what they were. Wisdom would have us persevere, confident that our choices were thorough and carefully considered in a painstaking process. It was time to realize we had no control over the future. The road would be long, and we had many more twists and turns to face, with uncertainty as our constant companion. But fear did not have to be. We were reminded of Paul's words to Timothy, in 1 Timothy 1:7, "For God did not give us a spirit of timidity (fear), but a spirit of power, love and self-discipline" (or as some translations tell us, of sound mind). This much was clear: we could only do our very best, as we had, and would need to leave the rest in God's capable hands. We stayed with the protocol, faced the circumstances as such, and put our faith in a loving, compassionate God. In the months and years that followed, I realized a refining work was taking place. It was a process that proved the need for constant surrender of our desires for the outcomes we wanted. We had to learn to make some life-altering decisions without knowing the final outcome, trusting God would be our constant.

Truth in Action

My husband and I, all these years later, still reflect on the agonizing decisions we faced during that time of our lives. We learned some valuable lessons along the way. Choices would always be a part of life; there was no getting around that. Just because we were Christ followers on a sojourn didn't mean the path would be free of rocks, boulders, and seemingly insurmountable impasses. If we were wise, though, we would do all we could to prepare for those possibilities. The choices we would make would reflect the preparations we had made beforehand. Part of the readying process was to learn to keep close to our shepherd, Jesus, who loved us enough to lay down His life for us.

One of the most familiar and well-loved Psalms, Psalm 23, became a favorite of my daughter's. In it, we learn that the Lord is our shepherd, and He will not leave us. A shepherd is the one who will leave the ninety-nine to go out, look for, and bring back the sheep that is lost—lost to fears, lost by choice, lost by accident. Nevertheless, Jesus will quiet our souls, as He cares for us. He gives comfort and peace, just like resting near quiet waters or in green pastures. We are told that at times, we will most certainly "walk through the valley of the shadow of death," but we don't need to fear evil of any kind. Fear of the future certainly falls into that category. So does fear of the past. The psalmist, David, tells us we need not fear because the Lord is with us. Even when we walk in the trials and sufferings of life, He is with us in them. The Psalm ends by telling us God actually 'prepares a table' before us in the presence of our enemies. When you prepare a table for anyone, is it not usually for some kind of nourishment, to sit and relax and even celebrate being together? That doesn't sound like a plan for evil; it sounds like a way being readied for our benefit. It sounds like the actions of a loving Savior and Shepherd tenderly caring for us even in the midst of our deepest sorrows. As we read the end of the Psalm, we see God's plan for us coming to fruition. He tells us, "I will dwell in the house of the Lord forever." These words have brought comfort to my family and me for the truth they bring. My prayer is they will speak to you in ways that will give you assurance and confidence in the one who can bring you safely through even the worst life puts in your path.

Reflection/Journal

~ 17 ~

The Character of God
Mary Rose

He got up and rebuked the wind and the raging waters; the storm
subsided, and all was calm. "Where is your faith?" He asked His
disciples.
—Luke 8:24-25

When in the midst of a storm, many of us allow what is circling
around us to entrap us. We put our focus on the trial and on all the
things that are being thrown at us instead of on Christ. The more we
do this, the more we allow doubt to creep in—doubt about who God
is. This, for many of us, leads us to begin questioning His character.

Over the years, as I have read this story from Luke 8:22-25,
one question in particular has stood out to me. For me, it lies in the
words of Christ, "Where is your faith?" In some ways, Christ may be
asking His disciples, "Do you not trust Me? Do you not have faith
in Me?" Personally, I feel the question goes a bit deeper. I think what
Jesus is asking them is, "Do you not know me? Do you not believe
I am who I say I am? I am your protector, savior, and provider. I
am in fact the embodiment of protection, salvation and provision."
I believe one of the hardest aspects for many of us when facing the
trials of life is holding onto who God is and knowing His character.
The more we slip away from the truth of who He is, the more we
doubt Him, and we begin to fear.

I have personally faced times in my life similar to this in which
the storm became my focus instead of God. One of these times was

during the years of my illness. Given the circumstances, I found it was more likely for me to focus on the physical and emotional pain that I was in rather than on Christ. As my mom began to see this happening, she realized I needed to hear and to be reminded of who God was. She began reading particularly the Psalms to me, many of which speak of God as our shield, our fortress, and our ever-present help in times of trouble. They speak of Him being our hope and joy and restoring us to peaceful waters. The more she read these, the more I began to focus my attention on Christ instead of the storm. We also began praying specific verses aloud and claiming their truth. In doing this, my mind was renewed and my heart was strengthened as I realized who I knew God to be.

I also began taking time for just God and me in the morning when I awoke and at night before I feel asleep. It was my time of tranquility with God. It was in those minutes and even hours that I talked to Him, poured my heart out and asked Him to remind me who He was and is. He would speak to my heart and mind by bringing to my memory the verses my mom and I had read. His character would be revealed to me. As He did this, He opened my eyes to see that in the depths of my heart I knew He was my best friend, my confidant, my comforter, and my daddy. Christ was my constant and still is, but at that time He truly became my hope. As I began to remember and understand more and more of the character of God, He then opened my eyes to something else. He showed me the ways He was blessing my family and me and how He was answering our prayers. As this happened, I was able to rejoice in the midst of my storm because God had remained the same, He was still sovereign. James 1:17 promises, "Every good and perfect gift is from above, coming down from the Father of the heavenly lights, who does not change like shifting shadows."

Truth in Action

Are the words of today true for you? Do you find yourself in a storm of life, and is your focus on the wind and waves and not on the one beside you? If this is you today, rest assured that not only has God not left you, but His character has also not changed. He is still and will always be your fortress, your redeemer, and your strength. Psalm 139: 10 reminds us that no matter where we find ourselves in life, no matter what circumstance we are facing, He will always be with us. It's God's character to never leave us. Not only will He always be with us, but He will also be our friend, our daddy, our hope, and our joy.

My challenge for you today is to pray and ask God to remind you of who He is. Carve out some time for you and Him. Find a quiet room of the house, your favorite chair to sit in or a patch of grass under a tree, and read the words of your heavenly Father. Open your Bible to Psalm 33, and allow His words to remind you of who He is. As you do this, you will see that He is the eye of the storm, your tranquility, and your constant. Allow your mind throughout the day to meditate on what you learned in your quiet time. As you do this, you will begin to see how He is working, blessing, and loving you through the storm. Know, too, that as you do this, it may appear as if God is changing, but He isn't. It is simply that you're learning the many different facets of God's character.

I also challenge you to find someone to help build you up, to be alongside you to encourage you to see and know the character of Christ. Whether the person is a family member, a close friend, or someone in the church, allow that person, whom you trust, to enter into your heart and help build your knowledge of God. If you are the one who is being called by God to do this for someone, have courage and know that God will give you the words to say, the encouragement to extend, and the love to pour out.

Reflection/Journal

~ 18 ~

Not of This World
Mary Rose

For our struggle is not against flesh and blood, but against the
rulers, against the authorities, against the spiritual forces of evil in
the heavenly realms.
—Ephesians 6:12

I believe there are times in our lives when the circumstances we find
ourselves in are not ones we ourselves can change. It's in these times
where the only one who can fight through and bring about progress
is God. For my family and me, we found ourselves in one of these
times in the fall of 1998.

I had been diagnosed with Lyme disease and placed on treatments.
The antibiotics were given through a pick line to provide a quicker
attack against the disease. For the most part, things were going as
the doctor had envisioned they would. Unfortunately, one specific
complication began to occur. My pick line would repeatedly fill
with blood. While the procedures my mom learned were generally
effective, on one particular night, my line would not clear. At about
12:30 in the morning, my parents rushed me to the hospital. For
several hours throughout the night, the nurses and doctors used
every method they knew to clear the line, yet nothing worked.

I can remember my parents entering and exiting the room. Each
time they returned, they appeared more distraught. At the time, I
didn't understand their heartbreak, but it was because I was not told
the severity of the situation.

It was a two-fold problem. The doctors were trying to clear the line using every method they knew, yet the more time went by without it clearing, the greater possibility of the blood forming a clot. If this happened, then the efforts to clear the line could possibly cause a clot to enter back through the line and into my heart.

The only things left to do that morning were to wait and to pray. Waiting was what we had to do, but time was what we feared we didn't have. I can remember my parents kneeling over my bed and begging God to clear the line and grant me life. Fervently and desperately they prayed this, along with many others that morning. The battle had turned from a physical fight to a spiritual one. We were left to trust that God was hearing our prayers and would answer them. The difficulty of this was we did not know if our prayers were in line with His will. Yet no matter the outcome, we had to believe God was in control and fighting the battle. As the minutes ticked by and an hour came to pass, God gave answer to our prayers.

Looking back on that morning, I can see how it was a pivotal point for my family and myself. My parents were placed in the situation of having to surrender to God. They had to surrender not only their desires but their daughter as well. It was a matter of saying, "Whatever it takes, Lord, do it. Ultimately not our will but Yours be done." It was through that experience God chose to grow my parents' faith and trust in Him. His ultimate purpose was for my parents to understand that despite everything happening, they could hold onto Him and trust in His will.

On the flip side, God used that morning to show me the reality of what we were all going through. I saw the heart of the battle, the truth of it. It wasn't just me fighting for my life, but my parents were fighting for it as well and fighting for our family's survival in the midst of it all. It was then I saw the incredible love my parents had for me as they were on bended knees crying out to God to spare my life. This vision will remain forever in my memory. It was in those moments that I turned from praying for my own life to praying for my parents. I prayed the outcome would be the best for them rather than for myself. Whatever it took, whatever they needed, and whatever would bring them comfort and hope, that's what I wanted more than my own life.

I believe God wanted us to learn what real sacrifice is: to love each other more than ourselves and our desires. He wanted us to trust in Him and know that when the situation was taken out of our hands, there was reason for it. The truth of the matter is, that morning was more of a spiritual battle than a physical one. God needed us to learn despite anything this world threw at us, we could trust in Him. He knew the battles that lay ahead for us, and we would need to be fully surrendered to Him in order to persevere.

Truth in Action

Are you facing a trying time in which despite everything you have done, nothing appears to be helping, and progress is not taking place? Perhaps you're in a situation similar to the one my parents and I found ourselves in that morning. It's in this place where you realize there is nothing else for you to do, and you really do not have control over the circumstance or the outcome. It can be a fearful time because all you're left with is waiting and hoping God is listening to your prayers. Let me assure you, if you have found yourself in this place, He is listening and there is hope. He assures us of this in Psalm 34:15.

As you wait and cling to His words, remember that this is the time when God can do His greatest work. It's when we surrender to Him and trust that His ways are the best that the real progress begins. Not every time will we be called to sit back and wait, but when we are asked to, we need to obey. It's in these times God knows the situation needs to be left in His hands. The reason for this is He knows when we do not have the strength to continue or are not ready for the fight. This realization is not a weakness; it's a reality. It's in our weakness that Christ's glory prevails and our faith is strengthened. We know this because 2 Corinthians 12:9 says, "But He said to me, 'My grace is sufficient for you for my power is made perfect in your weakness.'" So when Christ says to you, "Stop, pray, and wait," do it. Soon you will begin to see things in a different way, and His power will be evident to you.

Reflection/Journal

_____
_____
_____
_____
_____
_____
_____
_____
_____
_____
_____
_____
_____
_____
_____
_____
_____
_____
_____
_____
_____
_____
_____
_____
_____
_____
_____
_____

~ 19 ~

The Battle Is the Lord's
Marianne

David said to the Philistine (Goliath), "You come against me with
sword and spear and javelin, but I come against you in the name
of the Lord Almighty, the God of the armies of Israel, whom you
have defiled."
—1 Samuel 17:45

Another battle was being waged. This time the aim was different. My
son, my firstborn, was being put to the test. Our lives often felt like
a battlefield. It seemed we were constantly facing an enemy of sorts.
At times, I felt like a nurse in a battle who was running from person
to person in an effort to keep things going in the right direction.
Shortly after my daughter was diagnosed with Lyme disease, it was
suggested that the other family members be tested. It was often
the case that if one family member had been bitten by a tick and
infected, another had been also. Ticks aren't picky about who they
infect. Unfortunately, where one Lyme-infected tick resides, there
are usually many more like them, ready to feed on a human host.
The tests concluded that others of us had indeed been infected with
the disease. Jeremiah, our son, tested positive for Lyme.

Jeremiah, like his sister, had a love for the outdoors. My husband
and I had purposely striven to instill in our children a love for
nature. We weren't butterfly-catching, bug-collecting nature lovers.
We had the run-of-the-mill fondness for the beauty that could only
be found in the outdoors. When our children were young, we took

them to a church camp in mid Ohio. Long walks and talks about nature and how God existed there were all common. The kids had gone to camps through school. They had plenty of exposure to playing outside. It was the daily routine in the Takacs' household. We discovered, a little too late, there were areas nearby that were Lyme endemic.

The symptoms Jeremiah displayed were much milder than his sister experienced. Nevertheless, some of the telltale signs were there. He was to go in treatment for a brief time. It appeared things had been caught early enough for him. The battle for his physical health, however, was not the only one being waged.

As time and energy were being spent on my daughter, both of these precious commodities were not as plentiful for J, as some of his friends had begun to call him. I became concerned for him and prayed for someone who could be an adoptive mom for him. About that time, a friend asked how Jeremiah was doing. She had two boys of her own and said J could come over anytime he wanted or even needed to just get out of the house. As it turned out, my prayer was being answered. My friend told me of an agreement she had with my son so he could have the opportunity to have a change of scenery when needed without feeling like he would hurt my family or me or his sister's feelings. My friend let Jeremiah know he could call her quietly from anywhere in our house and let her know he wanted to come over. She, in turn, would call right back and ask him if he wanted to come hang out with the boys. Her sensitivity to not putting Jeremiah in a place where he was forced to say, "I just need to get out of here" or to have to lie that he was being invited over was amazing to me. I was so grateful to both her and God for giving Jeremiah this opportunity. Life at home was a bit stressful, to say the least, with a child who had a chronic illness requiring constant care.

I remember thinking, *Lord, what will become of my son?* The cry of my mother's heart became, *Please provide for him in ways my husband and I can't at this time in our lives.* I knew that at only eleven years old when his sister was diagnosed, a gap would most certainly exist, and I prayed fervently that God would minimize that gap as much as he possibly could. As twenty-four-hour care for my daughter turned into a full-time homeschooling job as well, more distance was created with Jeremiah. I felt the need to reach out to my son but at times was at a loss as to how. My days were spent with my daughter and his were at school, in sports, with friends or extended family, or in church activities. All of these out-of-the-house activities were very limited for me as I cared for our daughter to help minimize the medical costs on our already stretched budget. My son's life was being lived often without the needed attention of those that loved him the most. My heart broke watching as the years were passing and our relationship was becoming strained.

Over and over again, I found myself coming to a place of brokenheartedness for Jeremiah. At times I couldn't seem to muster the energy or courage to bridge the gap. It was during those moments of feeling lost over how to draw close to my son that I was led to reread the book of the Bible for which my son was named, Jeremiah. I was drawn to the words I found there, most especially the words of Jeremiah 29. As I read how God let the people know He had plans to prosper them, not to harm them, plans to give them a hope and a future, my heart was continually lifted and comforted. I had prayed those words over his life early on but needed to be reminded of their importance, especially as they pertained to the circumstances of the time. I prayed the words of Jeremiah 29:11-13 over my son's life. I knew it was one thing I could offer him consistently, my prayers for his future, for a hope, and for prosperity with the Lord. It was my deepest desire that no matter what battles he would face in his own life, he would be drawn to his knees and to the heart of God to find comfort, peace, and life abundant.

As time has passed, we have shared laughter and tears, joys and sorrows with both our son and our daughter. Our family has been in places of deep spiritual battle but never without the help of God, our Mighty Warrior. In a dream I had at the time, I heard the rustling of feathers, the clanking of swords and tin, and saw the presence of a warrior on a white horse in battle. The words impressed upon my mind were that my enemy had waged war against my family and me but that God was leading the battle against him. I imagine I will never forget that dream. It came at a time when not only were we fighting for the physical health of our daughter but also the spiritual well being of both of our children. The dream brought with it a renewed hope and peace to my heart. Although it has taken many years of consistent prayer, we have experienced the hand of a loving and faithful heavenly Father gently leading and restoring the relationships of our family. I have known the presence of the Lord was with us, guiding as we fought through the battles to come to a new place of closeness. I had to learn to trust in God's power and strength, not my own, because I would certainly not win the battle on my own.

Truth in Action

It's imperative when faced with a battle of any type that we know with certainty a few things to help guide us in the struggle. One of the best illustrations of a battle well fought is found in a Bible story most often read to children, the story of David and Goliath. If you look in the Bible in 1 Samuel 17, you'll find the story I am referring to. You may know David as the youngest son of Jesse, a man from Bethlehem in Judah. Jesses had eight sons in all, and the oldest three had gone to battle. David was assigned by his father to care for his brothers in battle. This was aside from David's job as a shepherd. The Bible tells us David arrived at the army camp just as the army was going out to its battle positions. The story states further that David ran from brother to brother in the lines, greeting them. He had supplies with him sent from their father. Get the sense of the nurse in battle I mentioned earlier?

As David made his rounds, the enemy that engaged the army, a nine-foot Philistine warrior dressed for battle, came out and showed himself. His aim was to intimidate them by his sheer size, hoping they would give up the battle before it even began, shirking back because of fear. Hmm, do you ever feel the enemy of your soul taking stands against you, ready to defeat you at any minute? Is the enemy the accuser who tries to cause you to give up the battle of a sin you can't seem to conquer? Is your giant the voice that belittles your every effort? Or is the voice your own, lying and saying you aren't good enough and never will be? Do you hear the shouts of Goliath trying to intimidate and distract you as you struggle to stand your ground and press forward? You must know who the true enemy is, the one who seeks to destroy you. The Bible says, "For forty days, the Philistine came forward every morning and evening and took his stand."

If we keep reading, we see David being so bold as to ask, "Who is this uncircumcised Philistine that he should defy the armies of the living God?" Furthermore, David convinced Saul, the leader of the army, that he, David, was the man to bring the enemy down. When Saul cast doubt upon David's ability, David retorted with his true accounts of facing and conquering lions and bears that came to destroy his father's flocks. I love David's tenacity and courage as he said, "The Lord who delivered me from the paw of the lion and the paw of the bear, will deliver me from the land of this Philistine." Saul granted him permission to face the giant. Ah-ha, the battle is on! Another important element you must remember in the battle is what David actually later tells us in Psalm 103:1-3, "Forget not his benefits." I have no doubt you, like I, have faced many previous battles. When you overcame them, who did you give credit to? You or God? If you are a Christian reading this, you know the truth of the answer. God has won many a battle for you, some you didn't even realize were being fought on your behalf. So why would He fail you now? Trust God, forget not His benefits, and let Him show Himself in the battle.

The story of David and Goliath doesn't end there. We are told David took his staff and put five smooth stones into a pouch and went out to face the giant. Goliath took one look at David's size, the fact that he was still young, and just about laughed him off the battlefield. "Am I a dog, that you come at me with sticks?" Further, he promised to feed David's body to the birds and animals. It's important to understand that the biggest battles we often face are the ones within us. We may look at a problem, the circumstances, or our own inadequacies and think, *I just can't win this battle. It's not possible.* Perhaps this is the truth you need to face: without God's help, His courage, His strength, and the faith He gives us, the battle won't be won. God tells us, just as He reminded Joshua, in Joshua 1:9, "Have I not commanded you? Be strong and courageous. Do not be terrified; do not be discouraged, for the Lord your God will be with you wherever you go." When you read the rest of the story of David and Goliath, you'll soon see what happens when we look to God to be our victor.

In reply to the scare tactics, the intimidation, and the lies of the enemy, David takes His stand with these words: "You come against me with sword and spear and javelin, but I come against you in the name of the Lord Almighty, the God of the armies of Israel, whom you have defiled. This day the Lord will hand you over to me, and I'll strike you down and cut off your head." David finished his declamation with, "All those gathered here will know that it is not by sword or spear that the Lord saves; for the *battle is the Lord's*, and he will give all of you into our hands." As we continue reading, we see David ran into battle against Goliath, and reaching into his bag to get a stone, he struck the Philistine on the forehead and killed him in one swift, fell swoop. God proved to be the victor! David's battle cry was to give God the glory. He knew whom he could trust and how to apply his faith to let God's power and strength win the war.

As you mull over and pray about this story and how it applies to you, remember this important fact: the battle is not yours, nor is it your enemy's. It's the Lord's. You will fight and be successful in the struggles you face as you recognize your true enemy, remember the battles already fought and won by a loving God, and have courage, relying on the Lord, the one who can win the battle for you as you trust in Him.

Reflection/Journal

~ 20 ~

Ask for Truth and Then Trust
Marianne

Then you will know the truth, and the truth will set you free.
—John 8:32

When you think of trust, what comes to mind? Is it the image of a person, someone you trust? Is it the idea that trust has to be earned? Or do you have a hard time even conceiving of trust, perhaps due in part to events of your life? No matter where your mind takes you on this subject, it's certain to make you ponder who or what it is you choose to put your trust in. Before you can trust in someone or something, there needs to be truth. Stop for a moment and ask God to show you what He wants you to learn about both truth and trust.

As children, our first models of trust are most generally our family members. Can you remember a time when you were facing a problem in childhood and someone in your family offered advice with the words, "Trust me, it'll all work out"? Oftentimes circumstances do work themselves out if given time and patience. But when we find ourselves trying to rush through a circumstance in order to get to the end of what we are facing, we can miss what we really need to learn. Inadvertently, we make the process last longer than it needs to. Has this ever been true in your life?

When our daughter was diagnosed with Lyme disease, my husband and I found ourselves wanting to fix things, to make it all go away as quickly as possible. The harder we worked to make it all better, the more frustrated we seemed to become. All of our running from doctor to doctor and between hospitals did virtually nothing to help us get to the truth of our daughter's health problems. In our particular circumstances, we could see the literal, physical results of improper diagnosis. I remember raging at God, demanding that He change our circumstances. He was quiet. This was even more maddening. At that time, I recall praying in desperation and asking where the problem was and what we needed to do to fix it. Finally, a gentle answer came to me: "Pray for truth to be revealed." That was all I needed to hear. I began to pray that simple prayer. All I could do was trust God would give us the answer we needed. Shortly thereafter, we had a correct diagnosis.

Finding the truth of our daughter's illness was only the beginning of a long process of learning to trust God. Oftentimes I found I did not want to hear the truth of what was happening. As it turned out, sometimes my trust levels were not there with God because of things others had done that caused me harm and left me not wanting to trust again. Other times my own foolish decisions left me in a bad place. Either way, learning to trust God and to ask for the truth was at first a painful and tedious process. But I discovered something along the way: the more I trusted God to bring me answers in His own time, the more I was able to continue to put my trust in Him.

As challenges were presented in the fight against Lyme disease, my emotions, strength, and sense of wellbeing were taxed. I had to learn to trust that God is who He says He is and His purposes are always good. Sometimes the truth I needed to hear dealt with forgiveness, sometimes rebellion, and other times anguish and denial. It became clear to me that real truth, truth that comes from God, is unchanging, just as God Himself is unchanging. Learning to continuously surrender myself to God was a vital lesson for me. I realized my emotions could not be trusted to tell me the truth about a situation. Instead, I had to learn to trust outside myself.

Learning to walk trusting in God was a new idea for me. I needed to understand I always had a choice with Him. He would be a perfect gentleman, never pushing or manipulating, just loving me until I was ready to listen to Him and let Him in. As my heart

softened and better choices were made, I found the truth easier to
hear, even welcome. While truth permeated my soul, trust was being
built. I continue to learn to trust in God and believe that no matter
what, God has my back. There is no better place to be than in the
place of knowing I can always trust God to tell me the truth and
His grace will be sufficient for every circumstance (2 Cor. 12:9).
These timeless truths, if you let them, will help transform you and
your thinking. Just as Paul tells us in Ephesians 4:23, we need "to be
made new in the attitude of [our] minds, and to put on the new self,
created to be like God in true righteousness and holiness."

Truth in Action

A friend told me the sooner I realized I needed to ask one specific
question when faced with painful or unwanted circumstances, the
quicker I would begin to see positive changes. The question? Put
simply, "God, what would You have me learn here?" coupled with a
request, "Please don't let me go through this without having learned
something." For some of you reading this, those words could be the
furthest thing from your desires. Read this paragraph again, but next
time, ask God to speak truth and trust into you as you read.

Are you facing a period in your life, perhaps not for the first
time, where you need to go deeper in your trust with God? You
could be facing new or ongoing circumstances. Either way, you
may need to hear truth from God. Whether truth is about people
or choices, the past or the present, rest assured God will lead you to
it. He tells us in His Word that He is the Truth, the Way, and the
Life, and that no one goes to the Father in heaven except by Him
(John 14:6). Do you need to reach a deeper understanding of that
for your own life? When you face yourself and your neediness, it can
be painful and scary. God knows where you are at, and He wants
to bring you truth about yourself and about Him. He wants you to
know the truth that He is completely trustworthy because of who
He is, not what He does for you. You are loved outrageously by God
no matter what you've done, where you've been, or what anyone else
has told you. Further, God's Word tells us in 1 John 4:18 that this

love, which is a perfect love, casts out all fear. So you don't have to fear hearing the truth from God or speaking the truth of your own heart to Him. We are also told in John 8:32 by Jesus Himself, "Then you will know the truth and the truth will set you free." Claim that truth; you need to embrace it. I pray you will take this step so you may experience the healing God longs to bring to your soul and the freedom spoken of in Galatians 5:1 that awaits you.

Reflection/Journal

~ 21 ~

He Has Already Won the Victory,
Part One
Mary Rose

Even though I walk through the valley of the shadow of death, I
will fear No evil; your rod and your staff, they comfort me. You
prepare a table before me in the presence of my enemies. You
anoint my head with oil; my cup overflows. Surely goodness and
love will follow me all the days of my life, and I will dwell in the
house of the Lord forever.
—Psalm 23:4-6

I was ten years old and told I would never walk again. In addition,
the pain in my stomach could not be touched even with morphine
or Demerol. I was helpless and could do nothing to make my body
better, and that is when the lies began. It was the voice of, *Just do it.
If you take the pills, it will end all of the pain and suffering. You won't
have to feel this anymore.* At first I disregarded the thoughts, but
slowly, I began to give them a second listen and pondered them in
my mind. Is it true if I end it, I will not suffer any longer?

The answers didn't come easily. The truth didn't scream into
my mind, but what I did have was the love of God reaching into
my life through others. My grandmother was able to recognize the
spiritual battle being waged against me, and with this understanding,
she fought the battle for me. In addition to the already exhausting
situation, I was becoming annoyed with her way of fighting the battle.

I would utter the words, "I would rather die. I wish I was dead." Every time I said, this my grandmother said the name Jesus. She sat by my bed and claimed I belong to Christ and that Satan had no hold over me. I now realize the reason I felt so frustrated toward her was because the battle was going on inside of me. Satan was telling me the lies while I was begging for truth and safety as a child.

I also didn't understand at that time that the real battle was for my life. Satan was trying to deceive me into thinking ending my life would bring about victory. What he was really trying to do was gain my soul back by convincing me that taking my own life was the route to freedom. Even though I had given my life to Christ at a young age, I still had to choose in those moments who I would live or die for.

After a short time, God showed me that if I ended my life, there would be no turning back; I could not be saved. As these truths echoed in my mind, I drew strength from Christ and realized I really did not want to take my own life. I knew my life belonged to Christ, and I wanted to remain with Him no matter what the journey would be.

Through this experience, God showed me that He made me, every fiber of my being, and everything within me. Psalm 139:13 reads, "For you created my inmost being; you knit me together in my mother's womb." This means God designed every fabric of our being, and He loves us beyond anything we can possibly imagine.

The love of our heavenly Father has often been compared to a parent's love. If you are a parent, then you know what I mean. For moms, the minute you're told your child is developing in your womb, love takes root and as you feel the baby's first kick, the love grows. For dads, it's when you first hold your baby boy or girl. You look into his or her little eyes and realize you never thought you could love someone so much. This love astounded you, did it not? Looking back to things now, I see the love of my grandmother as being that same type of sacrificial love. She would not leave me alone to face the battle for my soul.

For those of us who aren't parents, we still have the ability to love unconditionally. Perhaps this unconditional love is toward our parents, our significant other, or our best friend. We have all shared the

God-given gift of greatly loving dear ones. Yet, this love we have does not measure up to the incredible wonder that is God's love for us. His love reaches so deep that He sacrificed His only son for us for our sins to pay the penalty of death we deserved. Can you imagine sacrificing your own child for the sins of this world? I don't even have a child yet, and I can't imagine such a sacrifice. My point to highlighting this truth is to remind us that God loves us even in the depths of confusion and desperation. We are never too far gone for His love.

Truth in Action

Know that the enemy is real, and he prowls around like a roaring lion to try and devour us, but remember, he's just a lion. A friend told me the truth about older lions. They generally do not have teeth. An older lion, therefore, depends on intimidation. The enemy of our soul, the devil, roars at us with fears, anxiety, lies, and imitations of our own voice and God's, but he can't bite us. He cannot capture us, and we need not be afraid of his roar, because Christ is our protector. He will not let us succumb to these lies and fears, just as Psalm 55:16-18 tells us!

So if you are one who has struggled with thoughts of suicide, know your heavenly Father loves you beyond what you can hope for or comprehend. You are precious in His sight, and you are held in the palm of His hand. Your existence is not an accident, and your life, dear one, is worth living. God has incredible plans for you. Jeremiah 29:11-13 promises this. So when the lies are growing and the fears are becoming oppressive, know you hold the power of the living God inside of you and you can cast those lies out. The truth is you do not need to entertain the lies of Satan because with Christ you have authority over your thoughts. When you stand firm in Christ, you will be free. Galatians 5:1 reminds us we are to be free in Christ Jesus. That is why He came—to set the captives free! We can be free in Christ, mind, body, and soul, and He will bring healing to all three. We just have to ask Him to do it.

Reflection/Journal

~ 22 ~

The Rhythm of Life,
Part Two
Mary Rose

Where, O death is your victory? Where, O death is your sting?
—1 Corinthians 15:55

On a previous day, we talked about death, but more so we talked about suicide and not allowing Satan to deceive you into thinking it's a way out. Today I want us to look at some other facts about death. The truth is, we all will one day die a physical death. We don't know when, we don't know how, and we don't know where, yet we know it will come. The day, the hour, and the second will approach, and we will meet our end here on earth. My question for you is, have you ever felt or been close to death yourself and known that God saved you? I have. I have been in the situation where death was knocking at my door, and in these moments, I was not only terrified but I was also saddened.

I was eleven or twelve years old at the time, and my mom lifted me into bed just like every other night. We said a good night prayer, and as she walked out, the door hit the jamb and the battle began.

I lay there in my bed trying to get to sleep and couldn't. Unfortunately, at that time, sleep was filled with fear. I feared if I went to sleep I may not wake up and that my life would meet the end. This night in particular was the worst. It was unlike all the rest, and I felt as though I had to literally fight for my life. Satan's lies began, and I started to doubt. If I died, would I go to heaven or would Satan some how be able to grab hold of me before Jesus did? I feared this lie because the feelings of death were overcoming. It was oppressive. It was as though I felt the evil surrounding me and trying to pull me under into the darkness and into death. It was a battle of spiritual warfare and an attack from Satan; that is why I doubted and feared.

As this continued, I fought the sleep. I thought, *If I don't fall asleep, then I will be okay.* Shortly, I realized I had to fight against this battle. I began to pray to God and beg Him to rescue me from it. I told Him the fears I was having, and I pleaded with Him to give me one more day of life, one more chance to see my mom's face in the morning. I didn't want to leave my loved ones. "Not yet, not this soon," I told God.

It's amazing that only a year or so earlier I had thought of taking my own life and that this night I was begging God to give me more days. The night drew on, and for three or four more hours, I begged God to spare my life. I began to cry and sob while asking, pleading with God to give me one more day. I surrendered my life to Him again. As I did that, God showed me He was with me, and despite the fears, He loved me and heard my plea.

Eventually, the night grew to early morning, and I fell asleep. I can remember that morning as if it was yesterday. My mom came in, as she usually did, to wake me up, and upon her leaving my room to start breakfast, tears of joy and thanksgiving streamed down my face. I was alive! I was living and breathing, and I was not only given the gift of life, but I was given the gift of seeing my mom's face again. Oh, what a transforming moment in my life!

For me, the morning brought with it new life. It gave me strength and renewed my trust in God. I realized He had saved me. With that came the assurance Jesus had the power to heal me from the disease, and He was actively working. I do not know if that night was marked as my end here on earth. Perhaps it was, but because of my plea and the prayers of so many others, God chose to instead grant me continued life. One thing I know with absolute certainty is God can do anything. On the flip side, perhaps God allowed this night of fight to jump start my faith, because from that morning on

I knew Christ was with me. I knew He answered my prayers, and I knew I would be well again. He showed me from this experience He had been with me all along. I was being held in the palm of His fatherly hand, and I knew I was safe in Him. Psalm 138:7-8 assures me of this. After this point, I knew I wanted my life to be a written legacy to Him.

Truth in Action

My question today is simple: have you faced death? I don't mean physical death, I mean death to yourself. When we die to ourselves, we give up our lives, hopes, dreams, and desires to Christ. We submit our lives to Christ, and when we do this, we are given the gift of eternal life. Eternal life is not something we can achieve on our own accord. No matter how hard we work for it in life, we can't gain eternity by our own strength, will, or desire. We certainly can't buy it. It's as simple for us as Ephesians 2:8 says, "It is by grace you have been saved, through faith and this not from yourselves, it is the gift of God."

The promise doesn't end there, though. Christ doesn't only give us eternal life, but He also gives us a new life here on earth and meaning to our life. In Matthew 10:39 we read, "Whoever finds his life will lose it, and whoever loses his life for my sake will find it." Part of this new life in Christ is having the gift of God's forgiveness and grace. Yes, God forgives us of all the ways we have sinned. Then, by God's grace, we are set free and don't have to be bound by those old ways. Second Corinthians 5:17 assures us, "Therefore, if anyone is in Christ, he is a new creation; the old has gone, the new has come!" Does this mean we will never sin or mess up? No absolutely not, but it means that when we give our lives to Christ, we are given his power to overcome sin.

One of the biggest fears people express about accepting Christ is, "Will I lose myself if I have to give Him everything? Will I lose the fun in life?" The answer is no. When we lay everything down, good or bad, at the feet of Christ, He loves to make us happy. He does this either by allowing our original hopes to be made realities, or He creates wonderful new dreams within us. He is the author and originator of joy and laughter, after all!

So, if you have not invited Jesus into your heart and feel the nudge to do so, it is simple. Don't be afraid. There is no particular formula, and there are no set words. You can begin by verbally telling God you know you are a sinner and then ask Jesus to forgive you of your sins, to come in to your heart, to transform you and to lead your life. This prayer can be as long or short as you want it. The most important thing is to believe in your heart Jesus is the Son of God and to confess this out loud. Allow Him to control your life and heart. You can read more about this in Romans 10:9-10 and in 1 John 1:9. Baptism is the other part to being born again. In Mark 16:16, Jesus commanded His disciples to believe and be baptized as a part of their salvation. If you have not done these steps and feel God nudging you to do so, I say to you don't be afraid to let go and allow Him to transform you. As you choose to live your life for Christ, know He says to you, "Welcome home, dear one!"

If you are someone who has already accepted Christ but are facing insurmountable odds or that thorn in the flesh, know that Jesus has not left you. No matter the storms you are facing, you can forever claim the promise of Matthew 28:20: "And surely I am with you always, to the very end of the age." This verse has given me great comfort during my battles. It tells me that though I am but a vapor, Christ has been with me from the moment I accepted Him. He waits for us to give our burdens, our struggles, our fears, and our hopes to Him. So rest assured when you cry out to Him, He hears every plea of your heart, just as Psalm 18:6 says, "In my distress I called to the Lord, I cried to my God for help. From His temple He heard my voice; my cry came before Him, into His ears."

Reflection/Journal

_____

_____

_____

_____

_____

_____

_____

_____

_____

_____

_____

_____

_____

_____

_____

_____

_____

_____

_____

_____

_____

_____

_____

_____

_____

_____

_____

_____

_____

~ 23 ~

What Is There Besides Plan A?
Marianne

In my distress I called to the Lord; I cried to my God for help.
From His temple, He heard my voice; my cry came before Him,
into His ears.
—Psalm 18:6

So you have plan A all worked out. What happens, though, when
your plan A turns, unexpectedly, to plan B, a plan you are not
prepared to face? Such was the case with our family in 1998. Life
looked pretty promising. A job I had been hoping for was practically
dropped in my lap. My husband was working fairly steadily, which
was a blessing in itself in the construction business. Our children
were enjoying the new school they were in, and both were making
friends readily. The days ahead appeared to hold the promise of
good things yet to come. Without warning, however, a change of
direction was thrust into our path. The news we received about the
recent blood work our daughter had undergone indicated a serious,
perhaps life-threatening illness was taking hold of her body. Life as
we knew it came to a screeching halt shortly thereafter.

I felt a bit dazed in the immediate days and weeks after the
diagnosis and prognosis were given for Mary Rose's health. Much
of life became a bit of a blur. It was soon apparent we would need
to make some life-altering decisions. The job I had acquired would
need to be left behind so I could be with and care for my child. The

decision to do so was not hard initially. The implications financially and at times to my sanity were yet to be felt.

Although the changes that were happening were huge in magnitude, the deeper spiritual and emotional effects would only begin to surface with time. We didn't really have the luxury of evaluating what the impact would be to the family as we slowly moved from a family active in our community to one of solitude and isolation. Decisions were made out of necessity to only allow a select few people into our home. Mary Rose's physical health was too precarious to risk exposure to other possible illnesses.

In a short amount of time, my husband and I came to the realization that not only life as we knew it to be but also the directions we thought we would be headed for were not to become reality. My heart sank as the realities of the moment began to sink in. Moments of crying out to God, pleading for direction, often seemed futile. I had plenty of time to contemplate and question the events and happenings of our lives. It was gut wrenching to watch it all slip away. I hoped something of the past could be salvaged. This did not appear to be the case for the future.

Have you had those painful, life-changing experiences where it appears nothing of the past is salvageable? If you haven't, wisdom would tell you they will come. When you face those times of life, you may wonder what you did wrong to deserve this or how a loving God could allow such devastation. At the very least, you will probably question yourself and have the need to find some answers or perhaps see someone punished for an unexplainable atrocity. The exact answers you are looking for may not come soon or ever. In the quiet moments, though, when you are trying to rest and sleep eludes you, you may begin to hear a very quiet, very still voice deep within. The sound isn't audible, but nonetheless, it's real and definite. If you are listening carefully, you'll recognize it as the voice of God speaking words of comfort and truth to your soul. It was in those exact moments when I began to experience the love and compassion of God as never before.

As I watched the suffering of my then nine-year-old daughter, I cried to God to help me understand what good could possibly come of this. I remembered the verse in Romans 8:28 that all things will work out for good for those who love the Lord. *Wow! Seriously?* I thought in those moments. I distinctly remember raging at God, "You want me think about what good could come in the future? Well I want to know about the here and now." The verse in the Bible seemed so shallow and hollow. Those words were meant to comfort someone else, I further told God, not me. I was not ready to consider the truth of those words. So there was quiet as God patiently waited for me. Meanwhile, the battle within raged.

People suggested I try to sit, when I could, in my own time, and look at some of the psalms in the Bible. Reading through some of the words of the psalmist, David, crying out to God and seeking His help, I realized others had faced similar struggles to mine. I began to think about the words I was reading. Perhaps it would never make sense if I tried to figure out what was happening around me. Further, could my focus have gotten off of who God really is as, instead, I tried to make logical sense of the events of my life? If those things were true, then it stood to reason the direction God wanted to point me in was not so easily going to be found. I believed it to be true that God loved me and would take care of me, so why was I finding it so hard to trust Him now? To my way of reasoning, loving me meant He worked out the good I had planned for my life. When that wasn't the plan being laid out in front of me, I doubted God's love. I began to remember the words of Romans 8. The realization came to me that the definition of good wasn't spelled out. Was my interpretation of good even accurate? I also took note of the words, "For those that love Him [God]." Didn't that include me? I knew I had undoubtedly accepted God's love for me at age twenty-three, and in turn, by His grace, I chose to love the Lord. Even as I formed a new definition of good and a deeper understanding of God's love, I was beginning to see that the plan laid out before me, perhaps plan B, was one I needed to learn about. Ever so slowly, I began to ask God to show me what was meant by the words of Romans 8:28 as they pertained to my life.

Truth in Action

When life as you planned it takes a drastic turn in a new direction, where will you turn for help? If you're like most people, before the storm hits, you've had some time to learn through previous life events to whom you can turn for help. If you have turned to God, I'm here to remind you, you can trust Him now. Frequently throughout the Bible we see people crying out to God for help. Nowhere is this cry more poignant than in the Psalms. There are a few I turn to frequently when I am in the place of distress and perhaps feel myself somewhat sinking. Psalm 18:6 tells us, "In my distress I called out to the Lord; I cried to my God for help. From his temple, he heard my voice; my cry came before him, into his ears." Those words give me incredible hope. It was comforting to know that God, the Maker of heaven and earth, listens to my cry for help and my pleas go to His very ears. There is peace in knowing this. He will listen as you yell out in frustration, He will cry with you when that's all you can do, He will be quiet with you when silence is what you need, and He will love you through all of it.

It may be your time to learn something completely new about God's love for you and what *His* good looks like in your life. There are seasons of life that appear to end abruptly, but then there begins a time that looks much like an endless winter. Just like a long, cold winter, you may be in a time of turning within, learning to depend on the One who can understand your frustration and pain. He is the One who, when faced with His own crucifixion, was devastated to the point of pleading for a less painful road to take. If anyone can understand the agony of having to follow a path not desired, it's Jesus Christ. Jesus faced some of the same feelings you are perhaps feeling. Although He knew the greater good was at stake, the plan of salvation, it didn't stop Him from briefly desiring another route. Make no mistake, the plan of salvation as it played out for humanity was not God's desire for His Son, His only Son, but it was for His children, for the ultimate good of you and me. It was the only way for reconciliation to happen between sinful man and a perfect God. Ultimately, Jesus's choice was to submit to the plan. Maybe if we were to ask Jesus what His plan would have been, He would look us in the eyes and say, truthfully, humbly, but with a knowing in His voice, "Well, crucifixion was not at the top of the list." When you find yourself in one of those places where your plan A is not working out and doesn't look promising for the future, ask God to help you with the new directions of your life. It has been my experience that when a major change is happening in your life that you did not plan, let alone see coming, it is time to surrender your plans, ask for guidance, and learn to be very quiet as you wait on the one who will comfort and guide you. The process can be painful and tedious at times, but the things you will learn as you leave your plans in God's hand while asking for His will be invaluable.

Think back to the time leading up to and including the crucifixion of Jesus. It must have appeared to those watching the plan unfold as if God had lost control and was letting Satan have his way. We learned, eventually, that was the furthest thing from the truth. The followers of Christ had other plans. They most likely felt their plans changing drastically, or at the very least, they were taking on a very unexpected turn. Life as they knew it would never be the same. If truth be told, the plan for you and me, for everyone throughout time, included the events taking place and led to what was to be God's ultimate plan for redemption and reconciliation for every one of us.

My challenge for you is to not give up on God. Ask Him to help you hold on. In our circumstances, I knew I couldn't face the road alone, and I asked Jesus to hold onto me with everything He had as I learned to cling to Him. Look for the ways He may be trying to speak to you and comfort, guide, and renew you. Look to the community of family, friends, and others He has put in your life. Let His love become apparent to you in new and wonderful ways. In time, as you take each step on your new path, much like Jesus's disciples did, you will see the road you are on as less scary, less overwhelming. You don't have to rush. Take your time, but keep on going, one day, one hour, or one moment at a time. It may just be that the plans you have made, the plan A you so carefully labored over, are going to be redirected. Is it a plan B for your life, or is it maybe, just maybe, what you see as plan B is actually God's plan A for your life?

Reflection/Journal

~ 24 ~

The Hope in Plan B
Mary Rose

But the angel said to her, "Do not be afraid, Mary, you have found
favor with God." . . . "I am the Lord's servant," Mary answered.
"May it be to me as you have said." Then the angel left her.
—Luke 1:30, 38

I have grown to respect the life of Mary, the mother of Jesus, over
the years. Her great faith, her willingness, and her courage are all
qualities I admire and hope to attain. The truth about the qualities
Mary displays is they were most likely not natural to her but rather
achieved and developed at a price. I can pretty much assure you the
life Mary had imagined for herself was not one in which she would
bear the son of God. She almost certainly faced public disgrace as
the child she was impregnated with was not, by natural causes, her
future husband's. She had the role of being the earthly mother to
Christ with all of its trials and tribulations. Additionally, Mary had
to watch as the world rejected, whipped, and hung her Son to His
death.

I can't imagine having the life of Mary, but what I do know is
my life and the twists and turns it has taken. I, like Mary, have faced
some pivotal points in which I had to choose God's way or mine. I
have to say, God's plan has always been more difficult. It's usually
the least taken, and it's often come about in a time frame different
than what I thought it should be. Partially it's longer because I get
impatient, I get tired, and I get derailed. I have often taken myself

off the course that God has planned for my life. In those moments, my diversion, or just life in general, often lead to a plan B of some sort.

Throughout my illness, I experienced many times of the plan-B situation because plan A didn't work out. In the fall of 2000, my physical therapist told me I would never walk again. To a child of my age, that was inconceivable. I couldn't imagine living my life and not being able to walk. The blessing of her words was that it was the very thing that spurred me on to work toward walking again. For the first few weeks, I began by slowly standing on my own, and eventually I was able to take small steps.

The excitement I had and the joy my parents experienced by such a miracle was what we had all waited for. It was a blessing of encouragement and hope. Finally, things were headed upstream, or so we thought. After about four months of gaining my footing and working toward walking short distances, I began experiencing vertigo. As a result, within a couple of weeks, I was back in my wheelchair. My ability to maintain enough balance to walk was severely impaired. I remember feeling frustrated and angry and asking God why this was happening. I didn't know if I was relapsing. I didn't know if the medications were causing it. All I knew was that I was terrified.

After nearly six months of vertigo, my doctor recommended me to my current chiropractor. This chiropractor focuses not only on skeletal realignment but also on releasing the spasms in the muscles. After my first visit with him, he determined that my neck muscles had become so weakened by the Lyme over the years that deep spasms had settled in, causing the severe vertigo. After about six weeks of him working on the spasms and me doing exercises to strengthen my neck, the vertigo subsided. I was able to start walking again.

Looking back on that time now, I can see the bigger picture. At the time, all I could see was the storm rising up and the night becoming bleak. I felt nothing but fear, anger, and frustration because the relapse was not part of my plan. I assumed when I began walking again that things would only continue to get better. When it came to a screeching halt, I didn't know what to do. I didn't have a plan, but God did. My plan wouldn't have led me to the chiropractor I saw then and see to this day.

What we didn't understand, but God did, was the condition most of my muscles were in at that time. The Lyme had eaten away at my muscle tissue, leaving it severely weakened, atrophied, and with deep spasms. My chiropractor was able to detect the problems and gain a better understanding of what my body needed in order to heal.

Since that time, it has taken eleven years of chiropractic adjustments and a daily workout for my health to be where it is today. Even though I was scared and angry about my circumstances, if I had not faced that six-month relapse, I may not have the healing from the Lyme I do today.

God saw the big picture; I didn't. Just like Mary, I had to choose to look for God in the midst of plan B and to accept His plan even though I didn't understand it. God allowed for a difficult situation to happen in order to bring about years of healing. So if this is you today, know God has not abandoned you to an alternate plan B. He hears your cries of distress and is working on your behalf. As you hold to this promise, you will begin to see the blessings and the hope in the midst of plan B.

Truth in Action

Are you facing plan B in your life? The waters may seem murky, and the answers you're searching for are not coming quickly enough. Is your direction unclear? Are you standing in the midst of it all feeling hurt, broken, lost, maybe afraid, and angry? Maybe the job you have been working toward, the baby you and your husband have been trying to have, or perhaps the love you so desperately want to achieve feels unreachable. If this is you today, God wants to bring you hope from Psalm 37:3-6. Please take a moment and read it, soak it up, and know it to be true. Trust God when He says "Delight yourself in the Lord and He will give you the desires of your heart. Commit your way to the Lord; trust in Him and he will do this; He will make your righteousness shine like the dawn, the justice of your cause like the noonday sun" (Ps. 37:5-6).

Even though it is hard to hold onto this hope when facing plan B, we must. We must cling to the author of it, Christ. In holding onto Christ, we have to stop running from our plan B. It's easier to run, though, isn't it? When we run, we think we can avoid the pain, the work, and possibly the outcome, the one we are so terrified to meet. The truth is we can't really run from it. The more we run, the more we prolong things. Sooner or later, the inevitable plan B will happen. The irony is the longer we fight it, the more we miss out on what God has in store for us, the *blessings* He has prepared.

To stop running, we have to stop fighting for our plan, dream, or desire. We stop fighting when we are able to mourn the lost dream or plan and then surrender it to Christ. When we do this and are able to accept plan B, God is able to use plan B to bring about the best for us. This may mean plan B will lead us to actually achieving our dream in a whole different way than what we had planned. It may mean, after time, God will give our desire back, or it may mean He has something greater for us than what we could imagine.

I don't know what the answer is for you in this process. What I do know is God understands what you are facing, and He sees the future. So as you are able look at plan B and enter into it, ask God to grow you and help you to learn what He has for you to learn, see and experience.

Remember, plan B may not be as you had envisioned, but it will very likely be the path to bring about the best in your life. So hold firm to Psalm 40:1-3. In your quiet time today, breathe, cry, mourn, and let God heal and show you that He will get you through this time. His best for you is in the working.

Reflection/Journal

~ 25 ~

Praise from a Grateful Heart
Marianne

Brace yourself like a man; I will question you, and you shall
answer me.
—Job 38:3

As a small child, my parents instilled in me the need to say thank
you. It was pretty much a strict code in our house, one that garnered
chastisement if it wasn't readily offered when appropriate. I'm not
sure if, at a very young age, I completely understood what the
purpose was, but it was something we practiced. When I got a little
older, something about the expectation didn't settle well with me.
Being told to be thankful for something perhaps I didn't want or ask
for seemed contrary to the very reason for giving in the first place.
The obligatory thank you lacked sincerity and one very important
quality: gratefulness. Therein lies the difference between an act of
obligation and a truly thankful heart—gratefulness. Learning the
difference between the verbal act of a thanks and the genuinely
grateful heart was a lesson God wanted me to understand.

During the first years after my daughter was diagnosed with
Lyme disease, there would come plenty of opportunities to learn
lessons about being truly thankful. It started, really, when the doctor
gave us an actual diagnosis and thus a name to what had been
happening to our daughter. I remember the incredible thankfulness
in my heart because we were no longer stabbing in the dark, trying
to come up with answers. As I looked at the doctor with tears in my

eyes at what I had just heard, I remember feeling a gratefulness I had not known in a long time. Although it was painful and deeply heartbreaking to hear the truth, it was also welcome and freeing. After a long search with very little hope, I could finally look at things with a renewed sense of hope. My heart was grateful and in awe of how God had answered our prayers.

As trials continued to come our way, deeper levels of understanding thankfulness were to be revealed to my heart by God. As I surrendered myself to God and kept moving in a forward direction, I realized the thankfulness of my heart needed to become something much deeper. It was when I hit the point of being totally uncertain if my daughter would continue her life here on earth, or if it was time for her to go home to Jesus, that a soul search I had previously not known began. I not only was angry with God about how the events of my life were unfolding and the uncertainty of my daughter's future, but I also thought back to my own childhood. I was trying to see what I could glean from the past that would possibly help me through the present time. As I searched my mind for memories, and poured out my heart to God, I asked Him to reveal Himself to me. It was at this time I began to see God's presence in my life like never before. I knew, even as a young child living through the divorce of my parents, that something beyond myself existed. I remembered feeling it in my heart but not quite understanding what it meant.

As an adult, I was able to look at the events of my life and the things I was learning about God's character and start to make some sense of what I felt in my heart. A new awareness of what God's presence in my life looked like was growing. God was reaching out time and time again to reveal Himself to me. What an incredible thing, I thought, that the Creator of all things would want me to know Him intimately. It was then that I gained an awestruck wonder of the One who *knew me before I was even in my mother's womb,* as Psalm 139 explains. I no longer clung to just having an obligatory thanks for what God had done for me. I was being transformed with a gratefulness that filled my heart with praise for the very nature of God. Grappling with the past and present events, I had the eyes of my heart opened to see the truth about God, and it profoundly altered my view of what it meant to have a grateful heart of praise for my God. I could, and did, release my grip on my daughter's life. With that release came a peace I had never previously known. I knew no matter what the future held, my God was indeed an awesome God and would be working out the details. He didn't want me to worry about the past or for the future.

Truth in Action

Has your heart been broken over the events or circumstances you've faced in your life? If you are finding it hard to keep your heart from being hardened or ungrateful, ask God to renew your hope in Him. As you look at what you have faced, or perhaps are facing now, don't let your focus be on what's going on around you or on what God has or hasn't done for you, but rather focus on the character of God Himself. We have a choice about how to handle the things we face, and sometimes our character is sorely tested. It can even be the case when we are alone, when no one is around. Ask yourself who you are in relationship to God. Then ask God to show you who is He in relationship to you. If you have never read the story of Job in the Bible, turn to it now. If there were ever a man or woman who could possibly have reason to question God, it was Job.

Look closely at the story. What do you notice? Job knows God, and Job knows himself. He ultimately learns, however, God is so much more than the minuscule understanding Job had of Him. Job has slowly lost everything he has held dear in life, and his body is afflicted with sores, and he is about to hear from God. Think about these few words from Job 38:3-7: "Brace yourself like a man, I will question you, and you shall answer me. Where were you when I laid the earth's foundation? Tell me, if you understand. Who marked off its dimensions? Surely you know! Who stretched a measuring line across it? On what were its footings set, or who laid its cornerstone—while the morning stars sang together and all the angels shouted for joy?" God continues in verse 22, "Have you entered the storehouses of the snow or seen the storehouses of the hail?" and the questions continue for two chapters. God spoke truth to Job, and Job answered, "I am unworthy—how can I reply to you?

I put my hand over my mouth. I spoke once, but I have no answer—twice but I will say no more." He covers his mouth as he realizes the unfathomable awesomeness of who God is. He is left speechless and in awe. I have had a similar, but I consider much smaller, experience with God. The result was the same: I was left speechless. Ask God what all of this means for you. He will gladly make Himself known, and I guarantee you too will be in awe and speechless and will find you have a renewed heart of praise for God.

Reflection/Journal

~ 26 ~

Seventy Times Seven
Mary Rose

Get rid of all bitterness, rage and anger, brawling and slander, along with every form of malice. Be kind and compassionate to one another, forgiving each other, just as Christ God forgave you.
—Ephesians 4:31-32

Throughout our lives, each of us has either been hurt or has hurt someone. It may have been in a physical, spiritual, mental or emotional way, but no matter how we were wounded or how we wounded someone else, we are all left with the word *forgiveness*.

For many of us, this word is a difficult one to swallow, whether we are the one who was offended or we were in fact the offender.

There have been many times in my life when I have found myself on either side of forgiving. Sometimes it has been learning to forgive myself, and other times it has been forgiving the person who hurt me. During my illness, I faced different times of learning what forgiveness is and how to choose it rather than hold onto the pain. It wasn't always an easy lesson to learn, or put into action, but over time, I began to see why it is so crucial to me and the other person.

One of these times occurred as I started becoming ill. I had several friends at that time, many of whom were from school. Unfortunately, as my health declined and I was unable to continue going to school, I did not see them as frequently. For the first few months, certain friends would stop over from time to time, but eventually the visits grew fewer and far between. Out of the twenty or so friends I had, only about a handful stayed close. As a child, it was incredibly difficult for me to understand this. All I knew was I felt hurt, abandoned, and confused. The feeling of being alone grew even more present as my health took a turn for the worse and the friends who visited regularly were unable to come.

The doctors placed restrictions on visitation for about six to nine months since my health and my body were in critical condition. *With my immune system failing*, the possibility of me contracting even a cold could have ended my life. It was in this time that I grew to appreciate even more my friends who did stay close. They wrote letters, sent pictures, and called on the phone to talk. In these acts of reaching out, I saw their devotion and love for me, and this led me to treasure our friendships all the more and realize I wouldn't trade those friends for anything.

These friendships helped me to sit back and look at my previous friends in a new light. I came to understand why they were unable to stay and see me through my illness. For some, it was because of their own issues and difficulties, and for others, it was simply too scary to see me in the state I was in. The truth of the matter was we were all very young, and at that age, I couldn't truly blame them for not being there. Over time, as I came to understand these things, I was able to let go of the disappointment and pain and come to forgive them.

Yet, if I had not taken the time to reflect and allow God to bring me to this understanding, I am sure the unresolved hurt would have spilled over into my other friendships, causing strain and possibly severing a few of them. If I had chosen this path, the friends I was blessed with, and I myself, would have suffered a loss. Yet, by God's grace, forgiveness took place, which opened the door for deeper friendships to develop.

Since this time, I have had many friendships come and go. Some formed into deeper bonds and others held only for a period of time. Yet the ones developed during my illness still bear close connection. A few of them I only see periodically now, but when we do get together, we pick up right where we left off. As for others, they have remained close friends to this day. Looking back now, I can smile and see how God used a painful situation to bring about greater blessing, the gift of having true and close friendships.

Truth in Action

Perhaps today you are struggling with forgiving someone who hurt you. Maybe this person was a brother, a sister, a parent, a friend, or even a stranger. The offense could have possibly been done as an act of violence, infliction, or retaliation. Then again, it may have occurred because of hurt, anger, and feelings of rejection by someone else in their life and unfortunately, you got the brunt of their buried pain.

However, the pain this offense has caused you may be keeping you from forgiving that person. Possibly it's an offense you believe is unforgivable, or maybe you're afraid if you forgive, they won't face consequences. Therefore, holding the offense against the offender is what appears to be the best option. For many of us, we choose not to forgive because we believe by doing so, it will hurt the offender more and give us some sort of revenge. The only problem with this belief is that it is a lie. Christ does not call us to avenge. He instead calls us to love and forgive and leave the vengeance up to Him (Lev. 19:18; Heb. 10:30). The truth is, the more we hold onto the offense, the pain, and the anger, the more they eat away at our hearts and turn us bitter. As this happens, it will spill over into our other relationships and cause further destruction.

On the flip side, you may be the offender and it is guilt that is dragging you down. Perhaps this guilt stems from the sharp words you spoke, the path of life you never thought you would enter down, or the pushing away of anyone who gets close to you. Yet whatever the harm was that you caused, the ability to forgive yourself may be your struggle today. The saying, "The person you're hardest on is yourself" is usually true for most of us. When we're faced with the realization that we have wounded someone, we usually forget to forgive ourselves or withhold forgiveness from ourselves because we believe we don't deserve it. When we do this, we become angry and closed off to others for fear we will perhaps repeat the same mistakes.

Either way, no matter what side of the fence you are on, the ability to face your pain or guilt and own them is the beginning to forgiveness and healing. Doing this is not easy. In fact, depending on how deep the hurt goes or how guilty you feel, it may define how hard it will be. However, if you can take your hurt, guilt, and anger to Christ, they no longer define how hard the steps will be. Instead, Christ will define your steps the more you surrender and trust Him. As you do this, if you are the offended party, you will be more likely to face things for what they were, how they affected you at that time, and how they affect you now. If you are the offender, you will be better able to look at the reasons behind why you offended and wounded the person and then be able to slowly heal from and let go of your previous hurts and issues.

Remember, whether your learning to forgive yourself or another, Christ is your greatest example. In Matthew 26:28 we are reminded: "This is my blood of the covenant, which is poured out for many for the forgiveness of sins." The truth is we all fall short, and we all mess up. Christ paid for our sins, however, and we have been given His strength to forgive. So my challenge for you today is this: do not hold onto the hurt or guilt any longer, for it will only prolong God's process of healing and redemption for your life. Instead, go before the Lord and tell Him what is in your heart. Cry if you need to, mourn, yell even. Let yourself be real with God about your hurt or guilt, and as you do, the healing will begin and forgiveness will take root. Remember, Christ wants nothing more than for you to feel His soothing touch and know His power to redeem, restore, and reconcile. So let the pride or self-infliction go and instead let the Healer do His work in you. Be free today, my friend.

Reflection/Journal

_____
_____
_____
_____
_____
_____
_____
_____
_____
_____
_____
_____
_____
_____
_____
_____
_____
_____
_____
_____
_____
_____
_____
_____
_____
_____
_____
_____

~ 27 ~

The Truth of What One Says
Mary Rose

No temptation has seized you except what is common to man.
And God is faithful; He will not let you be tempted beyond what
you can bear. But when you are tempted, He will also provide a
way out so that you can stand up under it.
—1 Corinthians 10:13

Perhaps you have found yourself in a difficult situation and needed
words of encouragement but didn't get them. I can assure you from
firsthand experience that I have been in such a situation; the truth
is, we all have been. It is a difficult place because the person suffering
needs words that will uplift. Unfortunately, at times, people speak
words they believe will help, but instead they hurt and hinder.

Today's verse is a perfect example of what one might say to
another in a difficult circumstance, and instead of bringing hope, it
often brings confusion. I don't know if anyone has ever spoken these
words to you: "God never gives you more than you can handle."
Perhaps, upon reading this, you realized you have been the one to
speak these words. I also do not know the connotation in which the
words were spoken, but what I do know is how these words can cause
more damage than they do good.

I have personally had these words spoken to me a couple of times
in my life. Most of these instances were during my illness, one of
which I remember all too well. I was experiencing a heartbreaking
time of fighting my illness, and death was thought to be a definite

possibility. Both my mom and I needed hope and encouragement. We needed to be reminded that God was still in the midst of the chaos and He was still fighting on our behalf. However, encouragement was not what we received.

I do believe the person who said these words to my mom and me was trying to encourage us by saying what we were going through was not past what we could handle. Unfortunately, the spoken words didn't carry their intended meaning. They implied a whole different meaning. First, the implication was God did this to us. Second, it was as if the speaker was minimizing the overall circumstance. I say this because of how in the verse it's written: "God doesn't give you more than you can handle." The truth is He did not give the circumstance to my family and me. He did not cause the trial in our lives. God allowed the circumstance to happen, but He did not cause it to happen. Though He allowed it, it also did not mean that He loved us any less or that He wouldn't be with us in the midst of it. In fact, He was the only way we were able to get through it all and come out on the other side victorious.

The true meaning of this verse refers to something entirely different. A friend of my mom's actually explained the meaning of this verse. It refers to temptation in life, not the trials of life. Although I suspect people want to encourage others not to give up hope, perhaps the words of 1 Corinthians 10:13 are not the best choice for encouragement. From this experience, I have learned to encourage people to speak from their heart, remembering what brought them encouragement during their trying time. At times, when no words are found and none spoken, the presence of a friend is often what is needed and provides greater encouragement and hope.

Truth in Action

Are you someone who is going through a crisis of life where the end does not appear near and your heart is in need of encouragement? Have you received the comforting words you have needed, or have you been discouraged by words that were said to you? If you have been wounded, I would first like to say I am sorry. Second, I want to offer you words of encouragement. Know, my dear friend, God is with you in your circumstance. He has not given up, He is fighting on your behalf, and He loves you more than you will ever comprehend. He knows the sorrow and pain in your heart and the despair you feel in your mind, and He will bring you out of it. Psalm 78:52-53 speaks of this: "But He brought His people out like a flock; He led them like sheep through the desert. He guided them safely, so they were unafraid; but the sea engulfed their enemies."

As far as what to say to the person who spoke the words, the best advice I can give to you is for you to hold your tongue. Try not to say a word at first when someone says entirely the wrong thing. Wait and pray on it, and if the words spoken cut a cord in your heart, ask God to show you the right time to approach the person and explain how his or her words wounded you. Most of the time you will find when you do this, a light bulb will click on in the person's mind and the remorse in his or her eyes will be what soothes your heart.

If you are someone who has spoken words to encourage but are realizing they may not have carried your meaning, I say to you, go and make it right with that person. Explain your intended meaning, and apologize for the hurt you may have caused him or her. If you haven't spoken words yet but know of someone in a difficult situation who needs encouragement, pray about how best to encourage. Whatever heartbreaking circumstance he or she is facing, I urge you to consider your words carefully before speaking. Think of the time when you were in the thicket of life and what you needed to hear, what brought you encouragement, and what made you laugh or smile. Think about what reassured you that God was with you and did care. Then go and ask God to show you what to say to your friend who is struggling and trust that He will speak through you. God go with you!

Reflection/Journal

~ 28 ~

The Unspoken Bond
Mary Rose

For where two or three come together in my name, there am I
with them.
—Matthew 18:20

We all have been born into a family. For some of us, our family of
origin remains our family. For others, it is a foster or adopted family,
and still for many, it is a family of friends. No matter who plays the
role of our family, we are all in need of such unity and love. We
need our families to stand by us, to be our rock, the ones who love
and encourage us through the bad and rejoice and celebrate with
us in the good. Personally, I am a firm believer that no matter how
we ended up in the families we are a part of, it is not ultimately an
accident. It's not by happenstance. God loves families. He loves the
unity, the coming together and building up of each other that is
meant to take place within a family. He loves the family unit because
He created it, and He longs to use our families and us.

The enemy of our souls, however, has a different plan for us. He
seeks to divide and destroy our relationships and to break down our
love, concern, and compassion for each other. If he does this when
life is going somewhat smooth, how much more will he seek to do so
when life is difficult? In all reality, when we stop and think about it,
it is far easier for the enemy to divide us from our families when we
are facing difficult circumstances. Yet, as we depend on Christ and
His strength in the midst of our trials, we will be joined and unified

with our families. During my illness, I began to learn what the meaning of family was and is. I was blessed to have my immediate family by my side along with other family and friends.

This unity of family, however, did not come easily during my illness. With the financial strain, the complexity of the Lyme, and the overall stress of the situation, division of our family could have been our outcome. At the time, that realization was one I feared. I remember being ten years old and worrying that my family would fall apart in the midst of our tragedy. Many who knew us even doubted the survival of our family till the end, partially because we did not know what the end would bring. I can remember a specific conversation my dad and I had at that time. I was propped up in my hospital bed, and he was feeding me dinner. I looked up at him and paused. Glancing at me, he said, "What's wrong?" I paused again and then spoke. "Dad, what's going to happen to our family?" He sighed, and looking at me, said, "You know, the enemy wants to use this to tear this family apart, but the only thing this will do is bring us closer together. I promise you that."

These words that my father spoke brought great encouragement and hope to me that day and in the days and months that followed. They were the words I held to, the ones that for me spoke promise that no matter what we would face with my illness, our family would stay together. Not only would we be together, but we would be strengthened and brought closer together because of the situation. To have my dad be the one who spoke those words to me made it seem as if Christ Himself was speaking to me. I say this because my dad is a representation of Christ within our family. He is the spiritual head and the one we look to for strength in our family. It is the same strength given by Christ for all of us, His church.

Christ showed my family and me how, in the midst of a tragedy, He can and will hold families together. He infused us with His strength to fight through the days and come through them with victory. Victory did not always mean things were stress and problem free. We still argued and had our disagreements. There were occasions when the tension was so intense, unity was not so apparent or felt. What the victory meant was that Christ was our strength. He was the one who filled in the gap and unified us. He kept us going and together even when each of us had nothing left. Christ became the glue to our family.

Yet, without our surrender to and trust in Him, Christ couldn't have done such an amazing miracle. Individually, though, we had to decide if we were going to stay together and rely on God or let the circumstances determine our family's future. As each of us decided to rely on Christ, He was then able to unify us in a way none of us could have imagined. Despite the difficulties and our own mistakes, we were victorious because of Christ and our love for one another.

Since the years of battling my illness, my family and I have faced different challenges and obstacles as most families do. We have endured hardship and rejoiced in blessings. We have cried in mourning and still praised God for His constant faithfulness. Through all of life's challenges, we have remained a family united by Christ. Our love for one another has grown as deep rivers do, and our bond has been strengthened as the cords of a string make a rope.

Truth in Action

Perhaps these words you have read today speak of your life's reality. Maybe you and your family are facing hardship. A family member may be ill, your spouse may have lost a job, or your child, now a teenager or young adult, isn't the person you thought you raised. I do not know what your situation is today, but what I do know is that God is there to help you through. I know that God has given you your family for a reason, and that reason is to build each other up, not tear each other down. It is to give you love, not hatred and turmoil. It is to encourage you to press on and overcome the hardship together. I encourage you today to persevere. At times, during hardship, we all contemplate jumping ship. I say to you, don't do it. You will regret it, and it will be far more difficult and painful to heal. Additionally, I encourage you to make time for you and God. Ask Him to give you the strength to fight through and fight for your family's restoration and unity. Allow Him to refuel your tank and fill you with His joy, for His joy is our strength. Nehemiah 8:10 assures us of this.

As He gives you the strength to keep on, begin praying for your family as a whole and as individuals. Ask God to work in your hearts. Perhaps you and members of your family can sit down and discuss the difficulties you are facing and how best to work together for unity. One decision you will want to make united is the issue of failure not being an option. You must each decide to join in the fight for your family unity instead of allowing the enemy to use the circumstance to divide and destroy your family. Keep firmly in your minds that no matter what the difficulty, God can and will work to bring about healing, restoration, and unification. His glory will prevail if you seek Him first and keep Him as the center force. Philippians 4:13 states, "I can do everything through Him who gives me strength."

If you are someone reading this who is not facing family difficulty but have a friend who is, then I say to you, pray for your friend and his or her family. At times, you may feel as though prayer is not enough, but know that it is and that God hears the prayers of his people. Psalm 17:6 assures us of this. Encourage your friend to seek out God and rely on Him. Be there for your friend and his or her family in whatever ways God leads you to be. Also, ask God to show you His power and His glory at work in him or her. It will grow your faith and bring you greater hope and encouragement with whatever you may be facing in your life.

Reflection/Journal

_____

_____

_____

_____

_____

_____

_____

_____

_____

_____

_____

_____

_____

_____

_____

_____

_____

_____

_____

_____

_____

_____

_____

_____

_____

_____

~ 29 ~

Silent Night, Holy Night
Marianne

Glory to God in the highest, and on earth peace to men on whom
His favor rests.
—Luke 2:14

As I sit to write, I find myself in the midst of the busy, and at times hectic, Christmas season. All through the morning today, I keep hearing "Silent Night" in my head. The song takes me back to the quietness my soul wants to embrace, especially at this time of year. My mind wanders back to a Christmas of long ago. Though I'm not entirely sure what age I was, I remember a particular night watching my dad put up the manger scene on the mantle of our fireplace. I recall the white of the painted brick fireplace and of the cotton he placed around the nativity figures. Funny, it never seemed odd at the time to think of the manager scene being surrounded by snow. It was pretty, just the same, with the now old-fashioned colored lights, no longer in use, surrounding the edge of the mantle. I remember loving the spray snow on the windows. We taped stencils to the panes and used the pretty white spray to create a snowy look. Outside, the real snow came down in big white flakes, filling the yard with a fluffy wonder. What a peaceful hush there was to the moment. My father loved this time of year. I watched as he tirelessly worked to make our home a place of beauty and fun. The front door stood open as dad turned our door into a breathtaking package of shiny red with a bow like no other. The door was beckoning to neighbors and friends, as if to say, "Come inside the gift and see the wonder you will find."

As I look back on those memories, a longing comes with them. My father has been gone for ten years now, yet I find myself missing him and wanting to capture the simple wonder of those younger years. My daughter remembers how much Christmas meant to my dad and what a part it played in his life. No matter what the circumstances surrounding the family at the holidays, it was always my dad's desire for us to share in the joy of the traditions of the season. He loved the quietness and peace surrounding the midnight mass we attended on Christmas Eve. I could see the reverence in his eyes as he knelt in honor of the newborn King whose birth we celebrated. For me, this same point of connection is what draws me into the spirit of this time of year.

The Christmas season has always been a pivotal point for our family, even during the darkest days of my daughter's illness. When all else seemed uncertain and clearly not as it should be, the days leading up to December 25th brought with them quiet moments and memories to behold. Even in the most difficult times, when our house was quiet with an uneasy silence, God was working to bring a hope to our hearts. One of the years I will treasure most was when our pastor and his wife came to give a little Christmas sermon to our family. The compassion displayed in those moments spoke more loudly than any sermon or material gift had ever done. When I could not find peace in my heart or in the faces of my family, the kindness shown in our pastor's gift of himself brought the peace we all so desperately needed that year. It reminded me of my dad, who knew the value of seemingly simple gestures done without the expectation of receiving in return. We were left that year with a renewed sense of awe and reverence for the God whose birth we were celebrating.

Through the years, the place of gatherings may have changed, and the presents most certainly do, but the spirit of giving that is alive at Christmas is what always draws us together. It takes us to a place of quiet wonder. It is a place in our hearts where we can remember, draw strength from our shared experiences, and gain hope for the days to come. Some of the gifts of Christmas are just for us to enjoy, and others are to be given away. The good news of Jesus's birth is a gift to share with others. Just as my dad wrapped our front door to look like a gift to be opened, God wrapped His Son, Jesus, as His ultimate gift of love for us to experience. Don't miss the gift God has prepared for you. It's His most sacrificial gift of love. Just as He reached out some two thousand years ago and put a star in the sky to guide the wise men, so He reaches out today to touch the hearts of men. He waits in quiet wonder for us to stop and take notice and to enjoy the peace that transcends all understanding as we come to behold His Son.

Truth in Action

Is your heart longing for some measure of peace at this time of year? Are the lines too long in the stores, the money too little, and the desires too big? Often in our frenzied rush of the season, we lose the purpose of why we celebrate Christmas. Is it not to take time to remember a baby's birth, to dwell in the quietness that surrounds it, and to allow it to sink into our souls one more time? Isn't the idea behind Christmas to reach out to others, whether it is family we are estranged from, our neighbor, or someone who needs kindness? If you're having a hard time seeing the opportunities to pause in your busyness, perhaps you need to ask God to open your eyes to what He wants you to see.

Is it possible to find a measure of comfort in the memories of past Christmases? Maybe there is healing that needs to take place. The holidays can, unfortunately, be a time of unwelcome chaos and confusion. It isn't always a matter of coming out of the chaos but rather standing in the middle of it. Sometimes we need to have the understanding of our hearts opened rather than the circumstances of our lives changed. Only you can determine with God the place you need to be. There are many things I cannot tell you as definite for your holidays, but I can tell you this: God is waiting to meet with you. His Word promises a peace for your heart, one that is above our comprehension, as you give your cares, worries, and heartaches to Him (see Phil. 4:6-7; 1 Peter 5:7). He will meet you there. Don't miss the possibilities awaiting you in the celebration of the birth of our Savior. Read through some of the Bibles accounts of His birth, and reflect on the meaning behind such incredible love given in the form of a tiny baby so very long ago.

Reflection/Journal

_____
_____
_____
_____
_____
_____
_____
_____
_____
_____
_____
_____
_____
_____
_____
_____
_____
_____
_____
_____
_____
_____
_____
_____
_____

~ 30 ~

Finding Hope
Marianne

We wait in hope for the Lord; He is our help and our shield. In Him our hearts rejoice, for we trust in His holy name.
—Psalm 33:20-21

As perhaps, dear reader, you have noticed, not only has this book been about devotional time with God, but it's also been about the real life story of my daughter and I and our journeys. You've read about our heartaches, joys, and sufferings. But beyond the words and particular moments we've shared with you, we have the desire to instill in you a sense of hope and direction to help you find your place of peace. Our particular trials certainly are not new to the world, but our individual responses and the outcomes we've experienced most definitely are unique, as are yours. Every person has a story to tell. You might be thinking, *If only you knew*, or *You have no idea what I've faced*. While these statements are true, I imagine it's also fair to say I do know a little something about you. I know you, like me, like my daughter, may have had your own experience with seemingly impossible life challenges. You may even be facing such a time right now as you read the words written before you. I can also say with fair certainty that you may wonder where in the world your hope went—the hope you had for your future. While I won't try to predict the future for you, nor do I want, in any way, to minimize your experience, I do have a thing or two to share about hope.

In all honesty, I believe the idea of hope can sometimes be elusive. When living in the midst of crisis or chaos, the thought of having hope can totally evade us. I know it seemed like that for me many times throughout the years of my daughter's illness. All I could do, at times, was try to hang on for another breath to keep from drowning before the next tidal wave of events or emotions slammed against me with hurricane-like force. It can be dizzying to try to find stability, let alone even think there could be any hope. It may be that the source of your hope is yet to be found. It could be hard to discover if you're looking for it in someone who shares the circumstances with you. You may be aware that it is not wise to depend solely on those closest to you in the trials. You could possibly take each other down, rather than build one another up. Reaching out to those outside can also be exhausting. Every time you have to recount your story or catch someone up on the latest of the situation, it takes a little bit of the energy you don't have to give. Your prayers could seemingly be bouncing off heaven's walls, returning to you quicker than a boomerang. Does any of this sound familiar? Is it your story or that of someone close to you? As the words of many a contemporary Christian song tell us, we need to hold on because God is sending help for us

The hope you are looking for, the hope that gives reason to keep reaching your arm up out of the waters, is on its way. It may not seem like much of an encouragement at the moment, but don't dismiss the thought. The times when I have had the most doubt, fear, and discouragement are the ones that have led me to the place where I needed to be. The place of your greatest hopelessness is where you will find God's all-encompassing strength and His ensuing peace. It's the place you will find the hope you are looking for to keep going.

From the onset of symptoms with my daughter to the place of virtual immobility, a time span of three short months had passed. We were searching for answers, but there was no clear diagnosis. At that point, I cried out to God to give the answers we sought. I had to surrender my desire to not know the truth, to have the diagnosis be less than what it was. Soon thereafter, the correct diagnosis was given. We were able to move forward armed with the truth. God gave me hope in the form of truth. When the treatments she needed were so intense and things went horribly wrong, I was once again on my knees, this time surrendering my claim to my daughter's life. It was one of the most gut-wrenching things I have ever experienced. But it brought me to the place of openness with God. He, in turn, gave me hope in the encouraging words of the nurses who took care of my daughter. Eventually, as the months turned into years and it became obvious that we were permanently living in a new reality, God gave hope in the form of a "new normal," as our doctor always called it. I had to surrender my expectations for the life I wanted and eventually was able to embrace the life I was called to.

Life is yet full of new directions, some I'm not sure I always want to be heading in. Yet, I know the past is not a viable option, nor is the present the place God wants me to stand still in. He wants me and you to keep moving into the future. I've learned and continue to do so with circumstances I now face that my hope doesn't lie in other people, in life unfolding in the way I think it should be. It's not in the friends I have and not even to be found in my husband. While all of the people God blesses me with in life are treasures beyond compare, and the life God gives each day has beauty beyond measure, none of it can fill the deepest desires of my heart. In the same way, your loved ones and the life you've created won't be able to fulfill your longings or give you hope of a better tomorrow. The place of peace, and therefore your hope for the future, is found in God alone.

Only God remains the same. Only He can give you the security not to be found in others or in life itself. He can offer you this security because He is constant. His character is unchanging. He is not unsettled, as we often are, by the stresses, circumstances, and trials of life. People and events don't cause God to question His purposes for us, nor His plans. Our fears, questions, and doubts do not diminish God's love for us, nor do they cause Him to be thrown off course. He remains steady and true to Himself and to us. He has lived life here on earth facing the things we face each day, and He has conquered it all, including death. He will be the one you can hold fast to whatever life may bring, and His presence will be the anchor for your soul. He is the protector of your heart. Let Him show you how He wants to be all of this for you and more. My challenge to you is, what are you waiting for? What is stopping you from full surrender to the one who bought your soul at the cost of His life?

Truth in Action

Whether your life has extremely difficult circumstances, or even if you are in a time of relative serenity, be certain, your heart will only find hope for today and for the future in God. Check out what David says in Psalm 62:1-2, "My soul finds rest in God alone; my salvation comes from Him. He alone is my rock and my salvation; He is my fortress, I will never be shaken." Those are words to live by and cling to every day. He is the one who knows you best, to the point of having the hair on your head numbered, as His Word tells us. In Psalm 139, we read that God knew us before we were born. It's true. Discover it for yourself. Be certain of this: God has plans for you. His plans, as stated in Jeremiah 29:11-12, are to "prosper you and not to harm you, plans to give you hope and a future." You are no different than me, or my daughter, in that you will only discover that "hope and a future" when you purpose to come close to God. It's at this point of surrender that I find myself even today. The realization is that as I allow God to transform me, my heart is satisfied, and the contentment Paul talks about in Philippians 4:11, "For I have learned to be content whatever the circumstances," comes to be my reality and my hope.

Reflection/Journal

About the Authors

Marianne Takacs has a bachelor of arts degree in Spanish and is a professional life coach. Her roles as a homeschool teacher and a caregiver for her daughter have uniquely qualified her to instruct and inspire others in their life struggles. She established an emergency helps team at her home church (crossroadson23.com) in Ottawa Lake, Michigan. She now serves as a lay counselor. Her life experiences include spending a year in Antofagasta, Chile, serving on a women's ministry team at Crossroads, co-leading a mother-daughter Bible study for three years with Mary Rose, and growing older with her husband of twenty-five years! She has two grown children and makes her home with her husband, Randy, in Temperance, Michigan. You can visit her online at www.coachingwomenforlife.com.

Mary Rose Takacs has an associates of arts degree. She wrote for her college newspaper for a year and a half. She has received two MCCPA (Michigan Community College Press Association) awards and one college award for her writing. She is a recipient of an Excellence in Journalism award and won second place for In-Depth News Story in 2010. Her experience in fighting through an acute and chronic illness has given her an exceptional ability to encourage, comfort, and aid those facing traumatic circumstances. Mary Rose is one of the co-leaders of the young adult ministry, Cohesion, at her home church, Crossroads Community Church, of Ottawa Lake, Michigan. Additionally, she co-led with her mother a mother-daughter Bible study for three years. She currently makes her home in Temperance, Michigan.

Visit marianneandmaryrose at their authors' website, coming soon.

CPSIA information can be obtained at www.ICGtesting.com
Printed in the USA
BVOW02s1248220414

351246BV00002B/2/P